We Survived Infidelity

An Unexpected Life Lesson

Praise for We Survived Infidelity

"*We Survived Infidelity*, is a phenomenal love story of how God can transform even the most impossible situations into thriving, living examples of His grace. My heart ached with Hilarie in every turn of the page. I felt her pain as though I'd experienced it myself. Yet the hope offered even in the toughest, most brutal moments make this book a must-read for all couples striving to love each other the way God intends. Not only is it beautifully crafted, but the authentic, raw vulnerability offers helpful insight. I am certain this book will help countless people, many of whom feel like no one else understands. I am blown away at how God has worked in this couple's marriage."

— Jessica Brodie, editor of the South Carolina United Methodist Advocate

"If you are a woman who has been betrayed by your husband's sexual addiction and/or affair, this book will be a gift. Grab a cup of coffee and sit down with your new friend. Reading Hilarie's words is like going through her photo album, journal, and heart. Her transparency, along with her detailed description of the emotional rollercoaster, is heart wrenchingly accurate. Watching her path toward healing addresses many lies wives believe. Her story will prove you are not alone, assure you that you're not crazy, and give you many reasons to hope. She shines light not only on her process, but also on what was happening in her husband."

— Meg Wilson, author of *Hope After Betrayal*, founder and former CEO of Hope After Betrayal Ministries

"A fantastic read about a journey that no one wants to take yet many do. You'll be drawn in, you'll cry, laugh, cringe, and celebrate. And whether or not you have faced this journey, you will be challenged and encouraged in profound ways. There is ultimate joy and hope outside of yourself and even outside of the deepest of earthly relationships...this journey will lead you there."

— Dave Pacheco, lead pastor of Delaware Grace Church

"What a wonderful book. I was desperate for stories like this in the wake of my own D-Day. We Survived Infidelity will offer comfort and hope to many members of the club that none of us wanted to join."

— Elle Grant author of *Encyclopedia for the Betrayed* and founder of Betrayed Wives Club

I was deeply moved by Hilarie's ability to take the reader through her journey from relational tragedy to emotional healing and spiritual wholeness. This book will undoubtedly become a mainstay in the resources that are a testimony to what God can do with two broken individuals willing to submit to his amazing restoration and regeneration.

— Kirk S. Sharrock, Arbor Counseling, Columbus Ohio

"This courageous work will be both comfort and challenge for any woman who feels all alone in the devastating reality of infidelity. Hilarie's probing journal is an intimate walk on her personal journey into the searing pain of betrayal and the search for understanding. Along the way she shares her discovery of God's presence and the magnificent gift of His own voice to guide her through to personal healing and godly restoration of her marriage."

— Susan Allen, author of *The Healing Choice* and cofounder of Avenue Ministries

"Having walked this journey with Joe and Hilarie from the start, I believe their marriage is one of the best examples of infidelity recovery.infidelity. I greatly admire Hilarie for blazing a trail for other women to follow in processing this earthquake and allowing God to put the pieces back together again. I give the highest recommendation possible for this book as a help for women who find themselves faced with infidelity. I didn't just like it ... I loved it!!! The anguish they stumbled through as they tried to make sense of the heartbreak and the pain-filled moments, was riveting."

— John Doyel author and founder of 180 Recovery for Men

To be honest, I cried the whole way through. Hilarie's Life Lessons have so many parallels to our story and yet, seeing things through a different lens was nothing short of amazing. Her reflections and insights make me question myself in new ways, particularly with how I react to my husband's temptations, my triggers, and the micro-disclosures that trickle in like acid on my soul. Such a journey ahead still. But, after reading this book, I know that I am a different woman even today than I was yesterday. I have to be.

— Jen, Infidelity Care group member

We Survived Infidelity

An Unexpected Life Lesson

Hilarie Barry

Wind & Waves
Publishing

For my daughters and daughters-in-law,
Casey, Tiffany, Emily, Kelley, Tara, and Mandy.

So that you might understand.

May all of your life lessons bring you wisdom and love.

I love you girls.

We Survived Infidelity

PART IV

What happened to my life?

PART I

Chapter 1

Discovered

Two days before Christmas 2013, I sat in the dark at my daughter's oversized dining room table. Like a delicate ornament balanced on a tiny hook, my world teetered on the edge of all I believed, all that had seemed secure just that morning. I stared at the blank screen of my husband's phone and willed my finger to push the button.

I took a shaky breath and powered up the phone. The antique wall clock ticked as the phone glowed to life. I forced my trembling finger to swipe and tap.

"Messages" came up on the screen. "Cindy" shone bright at the top of the list, a harsh neon light in the middle of my peaceful, silent night. Blood pulsed in my ears. Tears welled. I couldn't breathe.

Wrong, wrong, wrong. All of this feels wrong.

Quickly, I tapped on the woman's name and scrolled through their text exchanges.

My heart stopped when I saw Joe's request and her response.

"I have to see you before I leave on my trip," my husband had texted. "Can I come over?"

"Yes."

***

Earlier that morning, back in Ohio, I pulled my long blond hair into a ponytail and slipped into my fuzzy coat. Soft Christmas music drifted from the speaker on the hutch in the living room. I heard Joe close a cupboard in the kitchen, and I called out, "Don't forget the Christmas cookies."

"They're already in the car," he said. "No way we're forgetting the cookies, and I promise I didn't eat any."

I gathered the pile of neatly wrapped gifts from the top of the piano and walked through the kitchen. Joe stood at attention, his blue eyes wide in mock innocence. "Well, maybe just one," he said.

Placing the gifts on the counter, I brushed crumbs from the corner of his mouth. "You better never stop running or all those cookies are gonna catch up with you," I said.

Joe was a fit man, and even with his shaven head, many people were surprised to learn he was fifty-seven. Recently, he had shaved off his neat, gray beard, insisting a clean chin made him look younger. I couldn't get used to his bare face. He didn't look like my Joe.

I picked up the gifts, stepped out the back door into the dark morning, and eased across the slippery deck. A light glowed in the trunk of the Malibu, illuminating an assortment of boxes and bags. Joe had left a space for the gifts beside my bulging suitcase. I'd packed everything I needed for the weeklong visit back east with my daughters Casey, Tiffany, and Emily. Joe bragged that he fit his things into a small gym bag—he would only be away for three days.

I slid the gifts into the space beside the suitcase. With the trunk loaded, the holiday scramble was over. I stepped away from the car to enjoy the pre-dawn silence. In the dark sky I recognized my three favorite twinkling stars of Orion's belt. I breathed in crisp, winter air and closed my eyes. Releasing the breath in a slow exhale, my shoulders sank, and peace washed over me.

Thunk. Joe closed the trunk. "Let's go, or are you planning to commune with Orion till the sun comes up?"

I shoved him playfully then danced over to the passenger door and climbed in.

Easing the car forward, Joe said, "Ready for an adventure, Babe?"

"You bet."

During my turn at the wheel, driving on Route 80 across Pennsylvania, I hummed Christmas songs and enjoyed the rolling, snow-covered countryside. The scenery reminded me of the card we'd sent to our family and friends. It featured a smiling snowman standing beside an old barn dripping with icicles.

Joe, oblivious to the winter scenery, leaned close to his phone intent on his text conversation.

I assumed it was one of the kids. "Who are you talking to?"

"It's just Cindy." His thumbs continued to dance across the screen. Cindy was a gal from our triathlon group, one of the people who Joe mentored. She'd been around for a while.

"What's she have to say?"

"Not much. She's just..." He hesitated and shifted in his seat.

I glanced at Joe, confused by his discomfort. "Just read it to me."

"It's a bit ... you sure you want to hear this?"

"Yeah," I nodded slowly. "Word for word."

"It's about her boyfriend, Max." Joe took a breath. "'Max is mad because now he knows I've slept with most of my friends.'"

I maneuvered the car around a truck laboring up the hill. "Why is she telling you that?"

"Well, I guess as a kid, Cindy's dad neglected her. Being her mentor, I'm like a father figure. She likes to ask my advice about things." Joe looked up and noticed the sign for Clearfield. "Hey, let's get off here, get something to eat, and then I'll take a turn at the wheel. Thanks for giving me a break with the driving."

I tapped the blinker and moved into the right lane.

"I'm starving, aren't you?" Joe said. "I can't believe how late it is. What do you want to eat?"

Cindy's text confused me, but obviously Joe didn't think much of it. He was more interested in food. I eased the car onto the exit ramp for Clearfield.

***

Joe and I married twelve years earlier, in our mid-forties. We lived in Ohio and had seven adult children from previous marriages. The kids were scattered around the country, with my three daughters living in the New York metropolitan area. My oldest, Casey, and her husband, Dan, had invited us to their house in New Jersey for Christmas. I would spend the rest of the week with Tiffany and Emily while Joe went back home for work.

That first night, we enjoyed a quiet evening sitting by the Christmas tree with Casey and Dan. The pine scent brought back wonderful memories of past family Christmases. Dan lit a fire in the fireplace, and I curled up on the couch beside Joe. Staring into the crackling flames made me drowsy after all the rushing around to get ready for our trip.

When the fire burned low, Joe and I climbed the stairs and settled into the guest room. The neat room felt comfortable with its new, plum-colored bedding. I opened my suitcase and took my bathroom supplies across the hall. When I returned, Joe lay in the bed, sound asleep. I climbed in beside him, a little disappointed that we hadn't gotten to review our day and kiss good night.

Warm and cozy under the heavy quilt, I stared at the primary-colored ceiling fan and wondered if Casey and Dan might have a child sleeping in this room one day. I turned off the bedside light and my mind wandered.

Tiffany, Ian, and their three boys would arrive tomorrow morning. Emily and her boyfriend planned to come later in the afternoon. I couldn't wait to make cutout cookies with the kids and spend time visiting with my girls.

My thoughts drifted back to our travels, and Joe's text from Cindy. "Max is mad because I've slept with most of my..."

No.

I sat up. *Joe and Cindy are friends. No way.*

My heart pounded. I slipped out of bed and felt around on the dresser for Joe's phone. I unplugged it and crept downstairs.

The phone, like a grenade in my hands, threatened to blow my world apart. I stared at the blank screen.

Please, no.

Chapter 2

Confrontation

"I have to see you before I leave on my trip."

No, no, no.

I dropped the phone and pushed back from the table. Bile rose in my throat, the bitterness on the back of my tongue made me gag.

Why? Why would he want to go to her house? What is going on? This can't be happening. I'm gonna be sick.

Panicked, my eyes darted around the dark room. My laptop leaned against the bottom step where I'd left it earlier in the day. I crossed the room, picked it up, and brought it to the table.

I'll write it down. I'll figure it out. I just have to write it down.

I lifted my shaking hands to the keyboard.

Monday December 23, 2013

I can't believe it. I'm sitting here trembling. I feel sick. For twelve years I have never once doubted I could trust Joe in all things. And now, I have a knot in my stomach. Blood is thrumming through my veins. Fear is making my whole body quake. Just writing about it makes my arms go numb. It's difficult for me to hit the correct keys with my hands shaking so badly.

Joe went to Cindy's house yesterday because he wanted to see her before he left on his trip? I don't even know what to think about that. Going over there is so weird.

I'm going to be here for a week, and he'll be going back to Ohio by himself. My thoughts are making me nauseous.

Should I just wait and see what happens? If I say something, he will be even sneakier. Even if there is "nothing" going on, there is "something" going on. Joe is involved with a woman who idolizes him and, in her own words, has slept with most of her friends. I don't know if anything will ever be the same. I am so scared. I don't know what any of this means.

The next morning, I didn't tell Joe I looked at his phone during the night.

I'm sure I'm wrong. He probably has a good explanation for going to Cindy's house. I'll look at his phone tonight and everything will be fine. I feel sick, but everything will be fine. I just misunderstood, that's all.

Joe, Casey, and I went for a three-mile run before breakfast. At least I tried to run. I hadn't slept all night and my stomach quivered. I developed cramps after two miles and was forced to walk the last mile.

When we got back to the house, Tiffany and her family were getting out of their car. Our three grandsons raced to us for hugs.

The youngest jumped up and down. "When are we gonna bake cookies, Mimi?"

I explained that my stomach was upset, so Tiffany offered to take over my baking duties. I promised to help decorate the cookies later. She herded the boys into the house. I followed and went upstairs to lie down.

Somewhat refreshed after a short nap, I ventured downstairs and joined the family. After nibbling at some lunch, I robotically decorated cookies with the boys.

"These are the best cookies ever, Mimi," Tommy said through a mouthful. He handed me a cookie. "Here, I made this one for you."

I took a small bite and my stomach roiled. The cookie tasted like cardboard, and I struggled to swallow it past the lump in my throat. Before I took a second bite, Tommy ran off and I snuck the cookie into the trash can.

The day dragged. All I could think about was Joe and Cindy—and why he went to her house.

Joe spent most of the day with his sons-in-law drinking beer and watching football. I stood in the doorway observing him joking with the men and noticed the yellow shirt stretched tight across his broad shoulders. A few weeks earlier he'd mentioned that someone told him he looked good in yellow. Was it Cindy?

Christmas preparations continued throughout the day and culminated with a reading of *'Twas the Night Before Christmas*. The boys hung stockings by the fireplace and were hurried up to bed.

Finally, at 9 p.m., I hugged my girls and went looking for Joe. I found him sitting alone in the den. When I walked in, he put his phone down and picked up his book.

"I'm gonna read one more chapter before I turn in," he said.

I gave him a halfhearted hug and dragged myself up to the guest room. I closed the door, muting the voices downstairs. My pulse raced.

Is he texting her right now? What are they saying?

I climbed into bed and pulled the heavy quilt up to my neck. The blanket did nothing to warm the dull chill inside of me. My stomach ached with tension. I lay shivering and stared at the ceiling fan. A childish thought flickered.

If I lay still, can I make it all go away?

Exhausted, my eyes drifted closed.

The click of the cell phone being plugged into the charger startled me awake. I listened to Joe move around the bedroom. My heart thundered in my chest. Afraid he would hear it, I turned on my side pretending to be asleep. He slipped into bed. The smell of his toothpaste made me queasy. I stared at the clock. The minutes crawled while I waited for him to fall asleep.

I'm wrong. Please, let me be wrong. Not Joe. Please—not Joe.

Joe's breathing slowed. I rolled gently to a sitting position and paused. The air in the room vibrated with the agitation of my waiting. The steady sound of Joe's exhalations continued. With my ears on high alert, I leaned away from the bed and stood. I unplugged his phone, moved across the hall into the small bathroom, and closed the door. I sank onto the thick rug with a muffled thud and powered up the phone. A few seconds later I found their most recent text conversation.

Joe: "It's been a long time since I've gone twenty-four hours without hearing from you."

No. No. No. My world splintered.

In a frenzy, I swiped through earlier conversations. Their messages went on and on with a scattering of affectionate endearments.

I don't understand. Why is he saying those things to her? He's supposed to love me. What is going on? I can't believe this.

I plunged into a place of shocked horror where nothing made sense.

I need Joe. I need him to fix this. Joe will know what to do.

I stumbled across the hall and pushed into the room. I stood in the doorway, unable to speak.

My laptop. I wrote it down. I'll show him.

I turned on the table lamp and grabbed my computer.

Joe rolled away from the light.

I tapped the keys and navigated to my journal entry from the previous night. I reached across the bed, grabbed Joe's shoulder, and shook him hard.

He turned toward me and pushed himself upright. "What's the matter, Babe?"

My mind went blank. No words came. The emotional overload was too much. I shoved my laptop into his hands.

Joe looked at me confused, then turned his attention to the screen and began reading. His body drooped as understanding dawned. I waited.

He said nothing.

I wanted him to fix it, to tell me I was wrong, that it had all been a mistake.

The room stilled, but only for a moment.

Like the tornado that had just swept through my world, I erupted into a flurry of motion. I grabbed Joe's car keys, slipped into my shoes, and ran out the door and down the stairs before he could stop me. No longer in control, I let the front door slam as a cyclone of fear engulfed me.

Run away. Home. I'm going home. I'm going back to Ohio. I need to get out of here. I can't stay here.

I shot into Joe's Malibu and backed out of the driveway, crashing onto the curb across the street. The grating of bumper on concrete resonated in the stillness of the quiet cul-de-sac. The angry sound matched the noise in my head, the spinning fury that had lay dormant all day. I slammed the car into drive and stomped on the gas.

I drove out of my daughter's neighborhood, yelling and cursing this man who was supposed to love me. The pain threatened to consume me. A high-pitched siren welled from deep within my chest, and I screamed. The sound pierced my ears, blocking the pain for a moment—an auditory reprieve from the chaos in my head. When my breath ran out, the silence hurt. Joe couldn't deny the words on his phone. He couldn't fix it.

I inhaled and let loose another deafening wail. My heart broke open, and the contents spilled out in an endless scream. I gave little thought to where I drove. The stores were closed, and there were few cars on the roads. I just drove.

And screamed.

Finally spent, I quieted. My ears rang in the abrupt silence. I continued driving. Numb. Empty. Alone.

I noticed a sign up ahead for Route 80, the highway that would take me back to Ohio.

Run away. Leave him. Yes, yes, turn here, go home.

I can't.

Yes, you can. Turn here.

No, no, this can't be right. I must have misunderstood.

You didn't misunderstand. The words were there. The words didn't lie. Joe did.

Approaching another sign indicating the entrance ramp for the highway, I held my breath...

And drove past the ramp.

I don't want the girls to know what he did. I'm not going to let him destroy our family.

I turned the car around and went back to the house.

Back to Joe.

I pulled to the curb in front of the house. Joe stood in the driveway, backlit by the cheery, white Christmas lights. When he approached the car, I couldn't read the expression on his shadowed face. It didn't matter. I was furious.

I rolled down the window. "Get in," I said and rolled it back up.

He opened the passenger door and climbed in like a disobedient child fearful of his parent's wrath. I didn't address him directly but drove, mumbling a barrage of angry accusations under my breath while he remained quiet.

I pulled into the empty parking lot of an abandoned supermarket. I drove around the lot unsure of where to park. The ache in my stomach swelled, and my body hummed like the flickering sign above the empty store. I parked, and we both stared at the darkened building.

When I spoke, the words came from a dark, ugly place deep inside that I never knew existed. I used profanity and called Joe names as I spewed my confusion and disbelief over the implication of what I read on his phone. Joe turned toward me, but his gaze wandered in the darkness outside the car. Anywhere but on the ravaged, hostile face of the woman he had betrayed. Given my naiveté and the overwhelming shock of his secret relationship with Cindy, my mind slid right past the possibility of a physical relationship, while my rage focused on the secrets and lies.

"You talked to her every day?" I couldn't believe it.

"Yes."

"Did you meet her places?"

"Mostly just at the Y."

"You brought coffee to her at the Y," I said. "I saw it in your text."

"Yes."

"Did she come to your office? People must think I'm such a fool. Did she bring things to you?"

"No."

"Why did you have to go to her house before we left?"

"I don't know," he said.

The interrogation continued for a time before dissolving into an angry tirade. I tried to convince Joe that his interactions with Cindy were wrong. As if his acknowledgment would erase all that had gone on.

"You shouldn't have texted her those things. You shouldn't have gone to her house. It's not okay for a married man to go to a single woman's house. What made you think that was okay? You know it wasn't right, don't you? You are supposed to be married to me and…"

He couldn't argue with what I said or what I saw on his phone.

"You're right." His head dropped.

"How long has this been going on?"

"A few months. We just got too close," he mumbled.

"It's called an emotional affair, Joe." I had no idea what that really meant but felt the need to label his behavior. "You've been having an emotional affair."

Joe's gaze shifted quickly to my face. "Oh, I—"

"Do you want to be with her?" My voice broke.

"No!" He scrubbed a hand over his face. "I want to be with you. I want you."

"Then why did you do this?"

"I don't know. I really don't know."

When my well of accusation ran dry, I shifted gears and listed all the disappointments I'd kept to myself over the years, things I had let slide because they'd seemed insignificant compared to the intimacy of the love we shared. Well, the intimacy was a lie—I knew that now. I wasn't Joe's cherished wife. Our entire past was a lie. And what about our future?

"Kelley just moved out. We're empty nesters," I yelled. "This was supposed to be our time together. You've ruined everything. Everything we were supposed to do together, just us. You've ruined it all."

I have no idea how long we sat in the parking lot. It felt like days. Nothing seemed real. My world turned upside down. The man I loved disappeared and took our marriage with him. A veil of numbness fell over me, protecting me from the full brunt of the pain.

At some point I turned the key in the ignition and drove back to the house.

In the guest room we lay side by side, without touching. Every few minutes I asked a question, he answered, and then silence filled the room. We lay, staring the ceiling fan until daylight.

Chapter 3

Christmas

The excited voices filtering up the stairs the next morning barely penetrated my fogged mind. I dressed with no attention to the process.

Joe watched me. "I don't know what to do," he said.

I pointed to the door. "Go downstairs and be the man you should have been all along. We've worked too hard to build this family. You'd better not mess it up."

He left, and I finished dressing, pasted a smile on my face, and dragged down the stairs to our Christmas celebration.

The girls were fixing breakfast in the kitchen.

"Mom, what happened last night?" Casey chuckled. "It sounded like you guys were fighting."

Tiffany carried a pan of eggs to the table. "Yeah, right. That'll be the day."

"I forgot my melatonin," I lied. "We went to get some. We had trouble finding a pharmacy that was open."

The girls laughed. Tiffany said, "See, Mom and Joe never fight about anything."

"I know," Casey said. "Dan says they have the perfect marriage."

After breakfast, the boys eagerly opened their gifts and then helped deliver presents to the adults. The gifts Joe and I had bought each other held no joy. Joe's eyes teared when he unrolled the poster I'd given him—a collage of photos from his Ironman Arizona triathlon. I now understood that the hours he'd spent training for the race included time spent with Cindy. Joe held up the collage when the boys asked to see it, then quickly returned it to its protective sleeve.

When the presents had all been opened, Joe and I carried our gifts up to our room. I lay my things on the dresser and turned to leave.

Joe held out a small box. "I have one more present for you." His hand shook.

"I don't want it," I said.

"Please open it."

He placed the gift in my hand. I stared at the silver package with the tiny red bow. I unwrapped the paper quickly and opened the box. In it lay a beautiful necklace with a diamond pendant.

Tears filled my eyes. I looked up at him and asked, "Why? Why would you buy me this if...?"

A tear ran down Joe's cheek. "I love you. I wanted to buy you something special for Christmas."

"You bought it because you felt guilty," I said. "I can't accept this."

I put the box in his hand and left the room.

I was numb through most of that day while holiday cheer buzzed around me. My emotions were scrambled, cycling through sadness, confusion, anger, and love. At one point I was filled with so much love for Joe, I was drawn to him as if by a magnet. I walked across the room and leaned in for a hug of comfort and reassurance.

Reassurance about what? That I was still whole?

I was far from whole, and a hug wouldn't fix anything. The comfort wasn't real. And the hug? Just another lie.

In a quiet moment, Joe showed me a text he wrote to Cindy and asked if he could send it. The message said, "Hilarie and I had a long discussion last night. I realize our friendship is more intimate than is appropriate for a married man. Even though it was never physical, it was essentially an emotional affair. I need to break it off for the sake of my marriage. I'm taking you off my contacts list and my Facebook friends."

I nodded. "Send it."

Five minutes later Joe handed me his phone.

A reply from Cindy: "Okay."

Relief flooded my body. I brought the phone to my chest, closed my eyes, and whispered, "It's over."

Throughout the day, I reread that message on Joe's phone many times. I took comfort in my belief that his text had flipped a switch. The crisis was over, finished, done. I believed we would be back to our old selves in a week or two. Everything was going to be okay.

I wish that had been true. There was no way for me to know that the nightmare had only just begun.

During a break in the action, I went up to the guest room to rest. My laptop lay on the table. I opened it and typed.

Wednesday, December 25, 2013
I'm afraid to begin writing. I'm afraid to open my frozen heart to the rush of emotion that is sure to break through if I allow myself to understand what's been going on in my life for ... how long? Joe said a few months. Joe has been having an emotional affair for a few months. I don't even know what that means. I'm numb. I just casually wrote that my husband has been having an emotional affair. I feel sick. Why did he need this?

I want to sweep it under the rug and curl up in his arms, so he can make everything okay. I want him to say all the loving things that let me know how much he cherishes me. I want him to protect me from this awful thing that has happened.

It is hard not to play games. I could tell him not to touch me. Then he would know how angry and hurt I am. But if I don't let him touch me, how will I be comforted?

I am going crazy. I think I understand the wife who goes back to her abusive husband. Who else can she turn to for love and comfort but the man who feels guilty enough to give it to her?

This was supposed to be my life with Joe. Everything I've looked forward to has been with Joe at the center. I thought I had the perfect life and the most amazing husband, and all along I have been sharing him with Cindy.

I shoved my laptop onto the nightstand, collapsed to the floor, and sobbed.

***

Joe had planned to take me to my daughter Emily's house the next day and then drive back to Ohio for work. Watching Emily and her boyfriend pack up their gifts that evening, I panicked. I couldn't spend another night staring at the ceiling fan. I had to go to Emily's house now.

I pulled Joe aside and shared my plan. He wanted me to stay until morning, but my mind was made up. I asked Emily to wait and ran upstairs to pack my things.

A half hour later, I squeezed into the back seat of Emily's car, unsure if my marriage would survive the week.

As the car pulled away, Joe stood in the driveway signing "I love you," his haunted face a mirror of my own tormented heart. The darkness hid tears that slid down my cheeks. I watched out the back window as Joe—and the life I thought we had—faded away.

At her house, Emily showed me into a tiny room that her boyfriend's daughters used when they visited, a perfect hideaway for the next few days. The dresser top was strewn with gently loved stuffed animals. The room was cool. A draft came from a large window that looked out onto the street.

I took a blanket from the pile on the back of the pullout couch, wrapped it around my shoulders, then carefully opened the couch, easing it against the dresser. I placed my suitcase on the bed and stretched out beside it, feeling nestled with my things so close.

I picked up my laptop and hugged it to my chest. My eyes filled. I had packed it at the last minute, planning to email Joe while I visited with the girls. Now, it would be my lifeline, a place to pour out my confusion.

How could I have been so wrong about my husband? Joe the Marine, strong, and courageous. Long ago he'd proclaimed himself my sheepdog, my protector. Joe vehemently criticized the wolves of this world for their lack of self-control. He barked about our family needing his protection. His mission was to safeguard all of us from the outside world. I loved thinking of him that way. I felt safe, knowing no danger would come to me while I was guarded by my powerful, confident husband, my sheepdog.

Now, like a wounded sheep, I cowered in the tiny room imagining my sheepdog with bloody wool dripping from his mouth.

A rush of fear-induced adrenaline surged through me, putting me on high-alert. Like a junkie, I wanted the high the adrenaline brought. It made me feel something after the numbing confusion of the past few days. A fight-or-flight response buzzed inside of me, but there was no one to fight and nowhere to flee.

My sheepdog had become the wolf, and I was terrified.

Chapter 4

Traumatized

The time I spent with Emily passed in a blur. She led and I followed, doing only what was necessary to appear normal. I decided to stop all communication with Joe for a time. No texts, phone calls, or emails. I needed to sort things out on my own—at least for now. My world was focused on the time I spent in the tiny room with my computer pouring out my pain through journaling and searching online, searching for something that made sense.

I've looked back at some of the articles I copied into Word documents that week, with no recollection of ever having read them. The shock of discovery offset any benefit I may have gotten from the information, but the articles at least let me know I wasn't alone in my horror. I wasn't the only one devastated by the discovery of a husband's relationship with another woman.

After two nights with Emily, I moved to Tiffany's house for the remainder of the week. That first night, I startled awake and squinted at the clock on my grandson's dresser. The red numbers glowed in the darkness: 1:38 a.m. I had been asleep for less than an hour.

I opened my laptop. The screen glared with words from my most recent google search: Experts generally agree it takes two to five years for a marriage to heal from an affair.

No way.

Being a statistic did not fit my plans. I knew that when I got home we would talk things through and everything would return to normal. Joe promised he would not see Cindy again, and I believed him.

I was unable to acknowledge the depths of primal agony that swelled in the pit of my being. I could almost convince myself that their relationship had just been harmless banter.

With my emotions hidden behind a numbing fog, the words I wrote in my journal read like deadened intellectualizing. My heart had died that week, and my writing could only skim the surface of my traumatization.

Friday, December 27, 2013
I can't loosen the tightness under my ribs and on into my stomach. Could that be a wall forming around my heart? Is that why I don't feel much of anything? It makes sense. I'm numb, but I believe everything will be okay. That's a good thing. If I stay angry and sad, I lose. If I keep beating Joe up, I get a browbeaten husband, a man who is less than he used to be. If I can let it go, I will find peace and have a man who loves me with a grateful heart. Memories of Cindy will fade. Maybe there is a role she will have played in our journey as a couple. I was afraid Joe ruined everything. That can't be right because what we have is too solid. He is just taking us through a rough spot. Maybe this whole thing is about his growth as a man moving into his later years. Maybe he needed a reality check to something I'm not aware of. At least it was just an "emotional" affair.

I just looked up emotional affair on Wikipedia. This is so much more than just texting: "The role of an emotional affair is to create emotional distance in the marriage. The unfaithful partner spends excessive time with someone they aren't married to. There is deception and secrecy, sexual and emotional chemistry, and denial."

Joe has been happy and upbeat because he is on an emotional high with Cindy. I liked him on that high. I thought it was because of this awesome life we created together, but it had nothing to do with me. He was excited about someone else.

He sounds different now. I'm sad to envision the broken man I will be going home to. I thought when I got home we'd talk and be back on track, but Joe won't be the same. Nothing will be the same.

I just want to get it over with. I want to go home and see what my damaged marriage is going to look like. I'm glad I figured this out before Joe had sex with her but… maybe it's already too late.

Each morning, despite the freezing temperatures, I went for a four-mile run. I needed to burn off the adrenaline-induced restlessness that had built during the night when I cycled between dozing, reading online articles, and writing.

During my four-day visit, I helped Tiffany with a major decluttering project, a perfect mindless task. We went through most of her closets and created large piles for Goodwill. I took home an extra suitcase full of hand-me-downs. For months after that trip I found articles of clothing in my closet and wondered where they came from.

The following winter, Tiffany stared at me in confusion when I asked if she'd left her leather coat at my house. "I gave that to you when you were visiting last Christmas. Don't you remember?"

No, I had no desire to remember anything from that Christmas.

On December 28, after two and a half days of silence, I lifted the communication ban and barraged Joe with emails starting at 4 a.m. I continued to email him at least once an hour until 10 a.m., when it was time to help clean out another closet.

In one email I wrote of my theories about his emotional affair. Another was paragraph after paragraph of questions. I sent articles about emotional affairs with lists of things he needed to do to break it off, the biggest requirement being no contact in any way, for any reason. I let him know that I couldn't eat, sleep, or cry. I just read and wrote.

Joe's emails were much shorter and less frenetic. He responded with apologies, answers to some of my questions, and assurances that it would never happen again.

One of Joe's emails:

December 28, 2013
Hi Babe,
*   I understand more each day what I did to you and I feel awful. I never intended to do it. I slid into the situation without realizing it. I hid one little thing, then more and more. I betrayed your trust and it just got easier.*
*   I want to hold you and love you, but I can't tell you it didn't happen. I CAN tell you it never will again. I look back at the last ten months and realize I'm not the man I thought I was. I have lost respect for myself.*

After you went to Emily's, Casey, Dan, and I spent the evening talking. Casey told me how much she thinks of our marriage, and how you think I walk on water. It was a knife in the gut. Dan chimed in to say we are like a storybook. What we have is tremendous. I wanted to blurt out, "You're wrong. I am a total ass."

I can't tell you enough how sorry I am. I am resolved to making myself a better man. I want to be the man you thought walked on water. I want to be your sheepdog again.

I love you Hil,
Joe

Prior to coming to New York, I had scheduled an afternoon visit with Rachel, an old teacher friend. I wanted to back out on the visit but decided the distraction might be good for me. I borrowed Tiffany's car and drove the ten minutes to Rachel's house.

Rachel was warm and welcoming and had obviously looked forward to our time together. She talked about her son's college experience.

"Jonathan is doing great at SUNY New Paltz. He loves his professors. You went to New Paltz for your master's, didn't you?"

I nodded, fearing I would cry if I tried to speak.

"He's planning to go out for track this spring. He always did well in the long jump in high school." She picked up a tray of cookies. "Here, have some."

I waved them away. Her cheerful enthusiasm was at odds with my agitation. I couldn't do it. I didn't have the energy to hold up my end of the conversation, and I couldn't listen to hers another minute.

She continued, "I love his new girlfriend. I really hope he—"

"Rachel," I said quietly. "I think I have to tell you something." I slid down in the chair and brought a hand up, covering my eyes. "Give me a second."

I burst into tears.

Rachel left the room and came back with a box of tissues. She put them in front of me and waited.

"I'm sorry," I said.

"No, you have nothing to be sorry about. Take your time. Are the girls okay?"

I nodded and continued to cry.

"It's not the girls," I stammered. "It's Joe. He—he had an emotional affair."

She came to my chair, wrapped her arms around me, and held me while I sobbed.

I told Rachel about my discovery. There were more questions than information. The two of us sorted through what little I knew and pieced together a new story, where Cindy really wasn't that interested in Joe. We decided that much of the affair had been in his mind.

I left Rachel's house lighter for having shared the burden of my secret and comforted by the new rendition of a one-sided emotional affair. From this new angle, our marriage appeared fixable. I was grateful for her loving support and not as fearful when I thought about going home in the morning.

The next day, New Year's Eve, Tiffany drove me to the airport. I had survived the week and kept my secrets.

Once the plane leveled off and the flight attendant cleared us to use electronic devices, I let down my seatback tray and opened my laptop.

Tuesday, December 31, 2013

I'm on the plane getting closer to Joe and I am going crazy. The squirrels are running around in my head. I can't stop thinking about Cindy and all the things I want to know. I was feeling okay from far away. Now I am going to be with him, and all the peace I started to feel is gone. It's like I'm in a bad movie where the wife thought she had the perfect life with her wonderful husband, then learns it was all a lie. The past year of our marriage has been a lie. Lots of lies that apparently got easier to tell. Why did he think that was okay? How did he justify it to himself with all our talk of having an honesty policy? I thought I was doing well, but I was just doing well from a distance. I should have known I couldn't walk back into my life like nothing happened. I've lost my best friend and I might never get him back.

I didn't want to cry on the plane, so I shifted my focus to an article I had downloaded the previous day. The words only fueled my agitation. The article was written about the effect of an emotional affair on the wayward spouse, the one who had cheated. It wasn't about me at all.

The author pointed out the hardships Joe would experience at the loss of his affair partner. He would have to grieve losing Cindy. The whole article was about Joe and Cindy and all that *they* had lost. The words felt like daggers.

What about me? What about my losses? I had lost my faithful husband and my dreams of our life together. I'd lost my past and my future.

The article said, "Give it time. It will take years to rebuild trust." How could I ever trust this man again? He had been having an emotional affair and I had to give *him* time to grieve? When would this nightmare end?

While on my layover at Philadelphia airport, I emailed Joe. He emailed back right away. His response made me want to vomit. All I could do was open my laptop and write.

He admits he's grieving Cindy, that it will take strength to resist contacting her. He said he'll have to look for other ways to fill that need. It infuriates me that this has to be about him. Everything I believed about my life is gone and HE is grieving.

It's time to get back on the plane. My life is a nightmare.

Chapter 5

Back Home with Joe

Three hours later, I swung my backpack onto my shoulder and moved through the jetway into the Columbus, Ohio, terminal. Fear made it difficult to put one foot in front of the other. The chatter from the loudspeaker announcing flights and lost passengers droned in the periphery of my awareness. My chest pulsed with anxiety. I willed my body forward, navigating through the crowd like a sleepwalker oblivious to my surroundings.

I saw Joe in the distance. He looked different, frightened. I had never known Joe to be afraid. My big strong man, my protector, appeared as fragile as I felt. He watched as I approached, then waited for me to make the first move.

I came to him, and out of habit we wrapped our arms around each other. Our hug was awkward, hesitant. After a moment, our bodies warmed with recognition, and we relaxed into the familiarity of holding each other.

Craving the comfort our hug provided, I melted into Joe's embrace. His chest trembled. Tears dampened my cheeks. We stood holding each other afraid to let go of this moment, knowing the next might be painful.

On the hour-long drive home the air between us cooled. Our discussion wasn't confrontational so much as clinical. I quietly asked the questions that had been burning inside of me. Joe's answers brought no comfort or order to my confusion. The bottom line? Joe had been having an emotional affair and he didn't know why.

I gave up on the conversation, adjusted my seat, and lay back, staring out into the dark sky. Just a week ago I had been married to my best friend and had the perfect life. While I was in New Jersey, all of that changed. My world turned upside down, and we were driving home to a life I didn't recognize.

I scanned the sky and was rewarded when I found three familiar stars. I brought my hand up to block the light coming from the dashboard and saw the entire constellation.

Yes, it's Orion. Orion is still here.

The stars brought me some comfort. At least something hadn't changed.

When I climbed under the covers that night, Joe stood beside the bed, as if unsure what to do. A week ago, I'd been repulsed by the idea of being intimate with him. I'd wanted him to hold me for comfort, but I wouldn't have let him touch me as a lover. Over the course of the week, however, my desire for Joe changed, and I now experienced a yearning to be with him sexually. My yearning didn't make sense. Nothing about this whole situation made sense.

Standing beside the bed, Joe waited for the verdict as if I were the judge. I guess that was the situation. In all our conversations we hadn't discussed sleeping arrangements. He timidly waited for direction.

I saw sorrow in his face. It mirrored my pain.

"Do you still want me, Joe?" I needed him to want me.

He raised his hands in a gesture of earnest confession. "I don't want anyone but you. I was stupid. I'm so sorry."

I looked into his eyes, trying to see beyond the words. I loved this man and believed he loved me, too.

"Show me you still want me," I whispered.

He climbed into bed and wrapped his arms around me. Our loving was both desperate and gentle.

After, I curled in his arms and silently cried myself to sleep.

***

The next day, New Year's Day, I woke with a start, surprised to be in my own bed with Joe's warm body pressed against my side. The intimacy of the night before had evaporated, and my heart pounded.

My mind swirled with questions, always more questions.

Joe sensed my agitation and turned over. "You okay?"

"There's more I want to know."

"All right," he said. "Give me a minute to wake up."

I got up and opened the blinds. A light dusting of snow covered the brown grass. The bare branches outside my window held no beauty this morning. They were stark, cold. A world turned ugly.

Joe lay with his head propped on one hand.

I walked back to the bed and sat on the far edge. "When did you first realize you liked her?" I asked, my tone light, almost conversational.

The question startled him. He sat up, adjusted his pillow, and leaned against the wall. Staring ahead he took a moment to answer. "I was attracted to her the first time we met."

"Did she come on to you, or the other way around?"

He took a breath and blew it out. "It was mutual. We liked talking to each other at the Y and run club."

"How do you know she liked you?"

"She asked me to friend her on Facebook. We started texting after that."

"Why did you encourage her?" An edge crept into my voice.

He shifted and readjusted his pillow, continuing to avoid eye contact. "I thought it was harmless. That it would never be more than a friendship.... I guess it felt good to be admired."

"Admired? Your texting went beyond that." I stood, my hands punctuating my words. "And what about the deleted messages? The whole month of November is missing. What was in those?"

"I don't know."

"What about our honesty policy, Joe?" I couldn't believe he'd been lying to me. "You always said we had an honesty policy. No lies."

Joe rolled out of bed and walked across the room. Placing both hands on the tall dresser, he stood with his head hung between his arms.

I followed, begging him to be the man I thought I knew. "Joe, you promised you'd always tell me the truth."

He remained quiet, eyes closed. His jaw trembled.

"Tell me the truth Joe," I pleaded gently. "What else did you say to her?"

A tear slid down his cheek. He took a shuddering breath.

"I slept with her." His voice was a whisper. "The first time was in May."

Something inside of me snapped.

I turned and strode across the room into my walk-in closet. I grabbed a pillow from the shelf and hugged it to my chest. The truth burst through the veil of denial that had protected me all week and shattered my heart. I slid down the wall, curled up like a small child, and sobbed.

Later, I straightened my cramped limbs and looked around the large closet that had become my sanctuary when our house was overrun with kids. Back then, this little space was my muted haven when I needed to be alone. Occasionally, I rested in my closet, stretched out on the floor with a pillow and my latest self-help book.

Now, laying on the floor, my thoughts were hazy, obscured by a numbing fog. *My husband had sex with another woman.* Even through the fog, ugly images swirled, and a new question took shape, overriding all the others.

I left the closet to find Joe. When I walked into the kitchen he froze. Without preamble I said, "Do I have to get checked for STDs?"

He lifted his glasses and slowly rubbed a hand across his eyes.

I held my breath.

"Yes," he said. His body sagged. "We'll make an appointment in the morning and I will go with you. I'm so sorry."

I nodded slowly. I had no more tears. I felt nothing, no sadness, no anger, nothing. I walked to Joe and leaned against him. He wrapped his arms around me and lay his head on mine.

PART II

Photos

The winter of 2014 was a difficult time of trying to understand what had happened to my world that had once been so peaceful and joyful.

1. Being out in nature gave me a momentary reprieve from the nightmare.

2. He said he loved me. Nothing made sense.

3. Sibling weekend opened a door I never expected. Here are Geordie, Lorna, Kenny, and me at a park in our hometown of Smithtown, NY. (January 18, 2014)

4. Joe and I took many "happy couple" selfies which I printed and placed all over the house. I was trying to convince myself that one day, I really would be happy again

Chapter 6

The Emotional Roller Coaster

Thursday, January 2, 2014

Can't sleep. Can't find peace. I just spent an hour searching on Joe's phone and computer. Searching for something. Answers, maybe? I want more information so I can make sense of what happened. Joe said he slept with her the first time in May, right before we went on a weekend bike trip with friends. I can't remember much about us that weekend. I'm trying so hard to remember. I can't find anything in my mind. He admits he spent the weekend thinking about her, and the affair continued after that.

I deleted the text on Joe's phone that ended his "emotional" affair. I had found comfort in what he wrote. Now I know he wrote it to deceive me into believing the affair hadn't been physical. That text was just one more in a long list of lies. Joe said it just got easier to lie to me. Will it always be easy for him to lie?

I'm confused by my physical desire for Joe. In My Husband's Affair is the Best Thing That Ever Happened to Me, *Anne Bercht says that most betrayed spouses go to one extreme or the other. They have either an insatiable desire for sex or are revolted by the thought of it. In the first case, the betrayed spouse may be comparing herself to the affair partner or she might be looking for comfort, for expressions of love, and to feel sexually attractive to her husband. I am not comparing myself to Cindy when I'm with Joe. I'm just looking for comfort.*

No, that's a lie. I am totally comparing myself to Cindy. I can't stop thinking about her when Joe and I are together. I want him to want me more.

Why can't I eat? Why does everything I put in my mouth feel and taste awful? I don't need to lose weight, but I am enjoying losing it. Why is that? Maybe it's because not eating is something I can control. Joe had an affair, and I can't make it go away. "I don't want to eat" is probably an extension of "I don't want to feel." I like the hunger ache. The pain lets me know I'm still here.

I know I need help, but who am I supposed to talk to? If I tell anyone, they won't understand. They'll tell me to leave Joe. Where would I go?

I got up from the kitchen table and stood at the sliding door. Snow had been falling for hours. The trees drooped under its weight. I slid the door open. The stillness beckoned me, calling me to come away from the nightmare. I shut the door and went to change my clothes.

Joe sat in the rocker by the bed. He put down his book. "What are you doing?"

"I'm going for a run." I went into my closet to change.

"Really?" Joe stood and went to the window. "It looks bad out there, and it's still snowing."

"I know." I zipped a windbreaker over my running jacket and slipped on heavy gloves.

"Maybe you should wait until the plows come through."

"I'll be okay." I knew Joe was right. It wasn't smart to run on the streets during a snowstorm, but at the moment my thoughts were more dangerous than the snowy roads.

I stepped out the back door and held out my arms. White crystals gathered on my sleeves. A world of tranquility lay before me, and my thoughts *still* revolved around Joe, Cindy, and the lies that made me feel foolish.

I wanted to escape the nightmare.

Moving to the street, I started a slow jog. The snow was deep, and my feet quickly became chilled. At the intersection, I turned onto a flat country road that ran through open fields. The wind picked up and snow stung my cheeks. I had to focus on maintaining my footing in what had now become a blizzard.

Once back on the main road, a car approached, and a sick thrill rose inside me. Can he even see me? *Maybe the car will slip off the road my way. It could all be over. No more pain.*

The car drove past, slowly.

I returned to the house safely. After I showered, Joe found me resting on the loveseat in our bedroom. He eased down and wrapped me in a gentle hug. I closed my eyes and relaxed in his arms. His warmth seeped into my body.

I felt him shudder and leaned away to look at him. Joe pulled me closer and broke into sobs. Shifting, he rested his head against my chest.

I stroked him as though he were a little boy. Between sobs, he spoke of his shame and his fear of losing me. I stayed quiet and held him while he cried. The pain had to come out. He needed to cry so he would be strong again one day.

Friday, January 3, 2014

Is it really only Jan 3rd? It feels like it should be the 10th by now. I'm exhausted from all the emotion.

When Joe got home from work today, I had a good cry. I told him he had been sick to keep going back to Cindy. He told me he always cherished me.

"No, you didn't," I said. "You were focused on her even when you were with me. You pretended to be focused on me, but you were always texting her. You cherished the sex and faked our marriage."

I cried and cried. A little later I was able to eat half a grilled cheese sandwich.

I continue to move in and out of denial with times of such painful sadness. It is easier for me to feel my pain with Joe holding me. It makes me more vulnerable to have my best friend, my abuser, there to witness my hurt. I do a lot of crying over the part I imagine I played in this. Blaming myself is probably just more denial. It's easier than crying over the affair itself.

Sunday, January 5, 2014

I feel like I am avoiding grieving. Joe suggested I may need to chip away around the edges of grief because that's all I can handle at the moment. He listened and supported me even though he was exhausted from his own reflections into his grieving heart. He is still my best friend. He wants to be my sheepdog again one day. Not right now. He doesn't feel safe.

We talked about how much time Joe spends on Facebook. Our intimacy got watered down by the attention and admiration he got from his Facebook friends. For years he has divided his attention between me and those other people. He got used to looking to them for entertainment and validation of his worth and prowess. Our family and I were no longer his primary focus. In the beginning, I think his relationship with Cindy was just an extension of his need for affirmation.

I feel like we are doing great together, but I just read this online: "Beware of the 'honeymoon stage.' A lot of betrayed couples go through a period of bliss right after they decide to 'work things out.' A sort of euphoria comes on, but it is simply false security, because the roller coaster ride often comes next. The happy honeymoon stage can last from two days to ten months, but eventually you will have to live in reality—tough times and all."

***

We were eating lunch that afternoon when I asked Joe to share his feelings about Cindy. I wanted to hear that the affair had been meaningless, an episode easily discarded. I wanted an assurance of safety.

"I'm angry at her," he admitted.

The tightness in my gut unclenched at his words. *Good, he's angry at her. He realizes she wasn't worth it. Okay, more. I want to hear more.*

"What do you mean?" I asked.

He leaned back in his chair and looked out the window. "I thought I was special to her. I wasn't."

I heard his pain. The tightness returned to my gut, but it didn't stop my words. "You wanted her to love you."

Joe's eyes welled. He glanced at me, then down at the table and nodded.

That single nod crushed me. I sank back in my chair and stared at the floor.

Why does he keep telling me things I don't want to hear? What if she had loved him? What if Joe had to choose between us? And what if he chose her or, maybe even worse, couldn't decide?

There was no way for Joe to derail the direction my thoughts were taking. I fell apart, again. We were both in agony as I spewed all the pain and anger running through my mind.

When the words stopped, the energy buzzing inside of me insisted that I move, that I do something. I went to the sink and began washing dishes. Joe made himself busy, tying trash bags, and sorting the recycling. I was only half aware that he was still by my side. My pain had not chased him away.

I think he was afraid to leave me.

Every day the rollercoaster of emotions dipped and rose unpredictably with soaring highs amid my darkest lows. Even in my anger I loved this man. He was willing to risk my wrath and work alongside me while my inner storm raged. How did he have the strength and courage to stand by me while dealing with his own demons and self-loathing? I wondered irrationally what I had done to deserve him. At this darkest time in our marriage somehow, I still saw the good in Joe. I wanted to love him, not berate him.

With the dishes done, I started working on the unopened mail. The mound on the counter had grown into a large pile since Christmas. I ripped open a few envelopes and stopped. Glancing at the papers in my hands, I shook my head, defeated.

"None of this matters," I said.

I swept the pile into the trashcan, walked into our bedroom, and closed the door.

Joe honored the closed door and went outside to shovel snow.

After that conversation about Cindy a painful ritual developed. Each morning, like a weatherman announcing another beautiful day, Joe proclaimed, "Today I choose you, Babe. Tomorrow looks pretty good, too." He would smile in quiet triumph, believing I would find comfort or possibly *even joy in his words.*

My mind raced each time. You choose me? Why is there a choice? You are married to me. You promised to love only me, and now there is a choice?

I didn't understand it back then. I do now. Joe fought a battle with his desire for Cindy. The claim, "Today I choose you," signified a triumph in the war between the desires of his heart and the desires of his flesh. Joe did not want his thoughts to be pulled from me, but the tug came from deep inside. A primal instinct to lust had been awakened long before we met. For him, controlling it was a victory, a triumph.

But to my naïve heart, my husband wasn't supposed to want anyone else, only me. I didn't think there should be a choice. I was wrong. We always have choices, and Joe made many bad ones.

When Joe said, "I choose you," it reminded me of all the times he had chosen her. I said nothing, and my heart wept.

***

The following Tuesday things were looking up. The STD testing had come back negative for both of us.

That evening I met Joe at his counselor's office. I hoped his counselor, Gary, would see me as a loving, supportive wife. I wanted him to convince Joe he was lucky to have me.

Joe and I walked into the office holding hands and sat together on the worn leather couch. Gary, a tall man with gray hair, had a slightly stooped posture. He introduced himself and explained that he didn't usually work with situations like ours, that his area of expertise was depression.

I remembered the thin workbook Joe showed me with exercises on depression. I found that confusing since we were dealing with infidelity. Now I understood why he'd been given the book and wondered if this was the right counselor for Joe.

Gary asked me how things were going. I told him we were moving along well and that, with his help, I knew we would get our marriage straightened out. I talked about the discussions Joe and I had about turning our life around and focusing on each other.

Apparently, Gary saw through my glazed smile and forced assurances. When I finished speaking, he asked, "What are you afraid will happen if you get angry?"

My smile faded. I glanced away and shrugged, shaking my head. "I'm not angry. Just sad." I turned to Joe. "It's your turn."

Eager to share, Joe didn't hesitate.

"I haven't thought about Cindy at all today. It's the first time in a long time." He shifted on the couch putting some space between us. "I try not to think about her, but I know her schedule. I think about where she is all day. We used to text when she had breaks." Looking pleased with himself, he added, "I'm just surprised I could put her out of my mind today. It felt good."

My chest tightened and my heart pounded as Joe's words about his obsession with Cindy's day, collided with Gary's question about my anger.

I know what will happen if I get angry. I won't be able to stop. I won't be able to control it. If I unleash the rage, the resulting pain will be excruciating. I will have to leave Joe. Every day there is something new. If I allow myself to feel, the pain might kill me. I would have to leave.

The ache of sexual betrayal is beyond description. The gnawing agony eats away at your heart. Betrayal was the choice Joe made to take everything he promised was mine and give it all away. Everything hurt. Each little thing he gave to Cindy wounded me.

How would I survive the mounting pile of horror?

Gary's question lit the fuse to my anger, and the pain of it simmered through my body.

We drove home in our separate cars. For the full forty minutes, I replayed Joe's apparent joy over not having thought about Cindy all day.

My anger burned.

He knows her schedule. He knows where she is all day. He thinks about her all day long remembering how they texted during her breaks. But today he didn't think about her and we should all be happy about that. I am so glad my husband took a day off from thinking about his affair partner.

When we got home, Joe followed me into the bedroom, and I let him have it. We stood on opposite sides of the bed, and I screamed at him.

With his hands in his pockets, he lowered his head like a beaten dog while I shouted a litany of ways he had let me down. I belittled him and crushed him with my words.

I became an ugly version of myself, and it scared me. I was a repulsive, out-of-control woman whom neither of us recognized. Unable to deny my accusations, Joe absorbed my fury in silence.

Chapter 7

Back to Work

I was early on my first day back to work after Christmas break. Walking through the empty halls of the elementary school building, I tried to reconnect with my old life. I loved being a teacher of children with special needs, but my world had changed. Now I felt fragile and jittery.

The sameness of my classroom surprised me. I picked up the crayons and paper scraps left from our last-minute holiday creations. Was it really just weeks ago that my students had worked around this table?

I walked to my desk and sat. I thought Joe and I would have this all straightened out by the time I went back to school. I believed my discovery would flip a switch and, poof, the affair would be over, and all would be forgiven. Now the betrayal loomed larger than I first imagined, and it consumed me.

Busses lined up outside the window. My two classroom aides stood beside the handicapped bus waiting to help our students. I heard the excited voices of children in the hall. When they entered the classroom, I felt flickers of the joy I used to know. I helped Suzy put away her lunchbox and reminded Ben to take out his communication notebook.

The nightmare receded. My shoulders relaxed. My teacher duties demanded that I be present to the needs of my students. One by one I directed the children to their learning tasks. They quieted into the familiar routines. We all settled into the predictability and structure of our schedule. I needed the structure even more than my students did.

My reprieve was short-lived. By midmorning, the internal chatter returned. I thought about Joe working just minutes from Cindy's home. Did he text her during her breaks? Did he meet her for lunch? Did he go to her house?

I couldn't focus on my lessons. I gave the kids simple tasks so they could work with minimal support. I sat with them to give the illusion of teaching and hoped no one noticed that I floated through my day. I had no enthusiasm and did only what was necessary. I kept my pain to myself and wondered how I would survive the next hour.

That Friday afternoon after a long three-day week at school, I practically crawled into the house. I took a diet cola out of the refrigerator, sat at the kitchen table, and opened my laptop.

Friday, January 10, 2014
I have been thinking of this as a challenge that will end. If I work really hard, getting by on little food and sleep, then I'll make it to the end, and it will all be over. But it won't. This will never not have happened. I will always be married to a man who cheated on me. I'm trying to eat again and that means I give up. My husband had an affair. I can't make it not true.
The fairytale is over. I was innocent in my love for this man. Joe always had the power to make everything in my world right. I had a childlike trust in our marriage and our vows. I believed I was loved and cherished, but my wonderful husband found Cindy's poisoned apple and took a bite. He fell under her spell and couldn't get enough of the beautiful witch. The fairy tale ends.
There is no happily ever after. I may find some happy, but I will always know that even my precious Joe can bring it all tumbling down and cause me pain like no one else. I'm being forced to grow up. Imagine, a fifty-seven-year-old woman finally growing up.

I closed my computer and stared out the sliding doors at the dreary winter scene. The snow had melted. The gray sky and bare trees were as lifeless as my emotions. Dead—my heart felt dead.

I watched a squirrel navigate the barren branches, leaping easily across space, confident of a sure landing. My eyes drifted from branch to branch with the squirrel, until a spark of clarity ignited in my brain, an answer to the question that haunted me from the beginning. My interrogations, the obsessive searching on his phone and computer, the hours and hours of writing, were all steeped in a burning desire to understand one thing. Why?

Why wasn't I enough? Why had he cheated? Why did he keep going back to her? Why does he still think about her? Why is our marriage balanced on the edge of craziness? Why didn't he love me enough to say, "No?" He called it "dancing with fire." Why? Why? Why?

The protective curtain of denial parted once again, and my heart lay exposed to the harsh glare of certainty. Joe cheated because sleeping with Cindy was more fun than sleeping with me. My mind spun in a freefall, twisting and turning in panic. Tumbling toward the abyss, I scrambled for something to hold onto.

Joe. My protector. My sheepdog.

I grabbed my phone and punched in his number.

He picked up on the second ring.

"I figured it out." My breath came in short gasps. "I know why!"

"What...?"

"You had an affair because sleeping with Cindy was more fun than sleeping with me." Hysteria edged into my voice, and I began to sob. "I don't know what to do with that."

"I'm coming home," Joe said.

I hung up, stumbled into my walk-in closet, and fell apart.

Forty minutes later Joe found me curled on the closet floor. I screamed and writhed like an animal in the throes of a death that couldn't come soon enough. Joe knelt, then lay down beside me. He wrapped his arms around me as tightly as my thrashing would allow. He couldn't quiet the storm he'd caused, but he hung on, determined to ride it out.

I apologized repeatedly for not being good enough, for not being the wife he wanted, for not being more fun. If I had only shown him how much I desired him, maybe he wouldn't have cheated. If I had loved him better, maybe he would have stayed with me.

The affair was all my fault. I wasn't good enough.

I pleaded with Joe to make it all stop. I begged him to take away the pain, to give me drugs, so I could sleep and never wake up.

I saturated his shoulders with tears and drool. Heavy mucus poured from my nose and throat. My chest heaved with my efforts to inhale. I blew my nose continuously but couldn't get ahead of the tears and gunk.

Seized by a rush of panic, I panted rapidly. Little air reached my lungs.

"I can't breathe," I choked out. "I'm suffocating."

"Sh-sh-sh," Joe soothed. "Slow breaths. Breathe slower, Babe. It wasn't your fault. I love you. Shhhh. You're gonna be okay." He held me, rubbing my head and back, trying to quiet my terror. The excruciating pain spilled out of my heart for more than three hours.

Joe never left my side.

When my wailing finally stopped and my panic subsided, Joe and I came together in desperate intimacy.

I tried to be "fun."

I wish the affair had been only about fun sex. I wish Joe's betrayal had been that simple. Over the next year, we learned that the causes of betrayal are complicated, and that Joe's brokenness began long before we met.

Days after my episode in the closet, my ribs still ached from the wailing and screaming, but the denial curtain had dropped back into place. I moved through my days like a sleepwalker, tuning in to the world around me only when I had to.

The following Thursday afternoon, Joe woke me from my fog with a short phone call. Realizing he had been only marginally focused on work during his affair, Joe had met with his boss to discuss changes he'd planned to make to tighten up his productivity. His boss listened without interruption, then explained that he'd planned to let Joe go that afternoon. After hearing Joe's improvement ideas, his boss decided to give him another chance.

"My timing couldn't have been better, Babe." Joe sounded almost giddy. "I really dodged a bullet."

He was relieved about work but clueless about my feelings. Joe felt lucky and I wanted to throw something.

I didn't know what to do with my anger, so I wrote.

Friday, January 17, 2014

Last night Joe said he had been "off his game" at work for six months—that makes it last summer. I'll bet he's been doing a lousy job for longer than that. What if he does lose his job? I can't stand this. Who is this man? Who is this man I have been trying to love after all he did to me? I am such an idiot. I'm the stupid one.

You know what? I don't trust Joe. I don't even know him. How can I possibly believe he will keep me safe when he almost just lost his job, putting me in the position of supporting him? We still have so far to go. What else don't I know about him? He needs to tell me everything.

I'm chomping at the bit to get back to my old life, or at least start my new life. I don't want to be in this crazy, obsessive phase where sadness, joy, and anger dance around in circles with each other.

I told Joe yesterday he could be my sheepdog again. Today I don't think that is such a good idea. He feels like he "dodged a bullet." He is feeling lucky. I feel like this is one more calamity his affair has dropped on my shoulders.

What happened to my wonderful husband? What other close calls will come out of this? Whoopee, Joe didn't lose his job, at least not today.

There is yucky stuff leaking out all over my life, and I can't stand it. I have to find a way to contain the mess. I need to put all of it in a box. Nothing fancy, just a stupid imaginary box with a hinged lid. I am going to take everything—the affair, Cindy, the texting, his job—and shove all of it in a box. That year of my life, when I didn't know about his betrayal, is over. As Joe tells me new things, I can put them in the stupid box. More information? There—it goes in the box. Joe's words can't hurt me anymore because I can close the lid and know it's over.

It doesn't do either of us any good to focus a lot of energy on the past year. Someday this will be behind us and I will just close the lid, put a big heavy lock on the latch, and know that part of our life is locked up tight. It has no part in today.

***

That weekend, I was scheduled to get together with my two brothers and my sister on Long Island, New York, where we had grown up. Prior to Joe's phone call, the plans for a sibling weekend held no interest for me. I didn't want to go. I was confused and afraid, and Joe had felt like my only grasp on sanity.

But now, hearing about the job he hadn't lost that day, my anger simmered. I needed to get out of Ohio, away from the never-ending nightmare. Joe couldn't provide the stability I needed.

I didn't know it at the time, but the visit with my siblings would alter the course of our journey. That weekend would nudge me onto a different path and lead us both in a new direction.

The day after "dodging the bullet," Joe drove me to the airport for my trip to New York. The weekend with my siblings provided a timely respite. We bundled up and visited our favorite beaches. We drove past our childhood home and reminisced about those days. We enjoyed silly bouts of uncontrolled laughter. The negative chatter in my head never ceased, but I chose to keep the nightmare to myself.

Our final day arrived, and my brother suggested we go to church. Both of my brothers attended regularly. My sister had her own eclectic variety of spirituality. At home, Joe attended weekly Catholic services, while I used Sundays to bike ride or walk in the woods. Church just wasn't my thing. Since my discovery, I'd accompanied Joe to his church but found nothing of value there. Formal religion held no interest for me.

But I agreed to go to church with my siblings that Sunday.

We drove a short distance from our hotel and pulled into the parking lot of what appeared to be a large warehouse. The building was nondescript and cold in its austerity. When we walked through the doors, the tone changed immediately. We were met with warm handshakes and eager smiles. Everyone seemed happy to be there and to have us visiting their church. We worked our way through the lobby and found four chairs together in the center of the large room.

I looked around, curious about this "church." It still reminded me of a warehouse with duct work and steel beams clearly visible overhead. Several instruments and microphones were positioned on a low stage at the front of the room. Behind that, a large wooden cross hung on the wall, the only indication that we were in a church.

The lights dimmed and joyful music filled the room. Everyone stood and sang with surprising enthusiasm. The atmosphere was that of a concert. I sang along, reading the lyrics projected at the front of the room. The music pushed all thoughts of Joe from my head.

The crowd clapped as the music ended, and a man walked onto the stage carrying a Bible. His neat but casual clothing was a startling contrast to the robes and formality of Joe's Catholic priest. Instead of leading us in ritualized prayers, he told a story about a man named Abram.

Apparently, God told Abram to pack up his family and his possessions and to leave his home. Abram did as he was instructed, with no idea where God intended him to go. We were asked to imagine ourselves in that situation, loading all our possessions into an SUV and leaving home with no plan or destination. Just faith.

"Do you trust God with your journey?" the man asked. "Do you give God control of your life, or do you insist on doing things your own way?"

The question made me think. I was like Abram, with no idea where I was going or what would happen next. Abram just did what God told him to do.

Could that work for me and my mess? Would God tell me what to do?

That afternoon, I hugged my brothers and sister goodbye and walked toward the plane that would take me back to Joe, back to my never-ending nightmare.

Chapter 8

Forgiveness

A week later, I sat at the kitchen table at 4 a.m. trying to process the conversation I'd had with Joe the previous evening. It had been a rollercoaster week. At the airport, my emotions soared when Joe lovingly welcomed me home, only to plummet that night when images of his affair played out in an endless loop behind my closed eye lids. Each day, sadness climbed toward hope, plummeted into despair and swept around sharply winding curves of confusion. This evening I experienced a swift ascent into forgiveness and wanted to explore it further.

Friday, January 24, 2014

Tonight, I told Joe I forgive him. But what does that mean? Online it said forgiveness is a decision to release feelings of resentment and anger toward someone. This could be a little complicated. I don't want to block my feelings of anger if they need to come out. Maybe the decision to release feelings means to feel them and then let them go. I can get angry, but I don't want to stay angry.

Forgiveness, for me, is based on understanding what happened and watching how Joe acts now. It's really a head game with myself. I hate what he did, but he's changed and rededicated himself to me and our marriage.

I can hear the "but" as I write. "But" is a demon I have to come to terms with. "But" he was very good at lying to me. For nearly a year, all the love he gave me was tainted with deceit. Does love still count when it is coated with lies? And what about the ones he told himself?

I circle back around to forgiveness. I love Joe. He was never the guy in that stupid box. Based on the man I have seen since December 23, I choose to forgive him and love him like no one else. I want to trust Joe with my heart again, a little bit at a time.

The next day, Joe chopped vegetables for salad, while I poured pasta into a bowl. I heard the tone of a text coming into his phone. He picked it up and read the text aloud, a new practice to help me avoid phone-related triggers. Sometimes just hearing the chime of Joe's phone transported me back to that first night of discovery. When triggered, my heart raced, and trembling spread through my body. I couldn't control the onslaught of fear when the trauma was reignited, and Joe did what he could to avoid causing me more distress.

The text came from Bob, one of the men in our triathlon group. Joe had told him about his affair, and Bob wanted to know if Joe planned to continue leading the group. He said it sounded like Cindy still considered herself a member.

I liked being with our triathlon friends, but the thought of running into Cindy scared me. Joe suggested that he and I could be co-leaders and attend all workouts and gatherings together. We could reconnect with everyone by throwing a party at our house. That would ensure Cindy wouldn't show up.

I carried the pasta to the table, and we made plans for the party while we ate. Maybe we could keep our triathlon group, after all.

The following day I awoke with more energy than usual. I was nervous about memories the party might spark, but I looked forward to having our friends come to our house. I carried my laptop to the kitchen table. Joe had a Facebook page for our group. I wanted to block Cindy so we could post an invite without seeing her name pop up. I didn't have much experience with Facebook, but how hard could it be?

Opening the site, I found pictures of my grandsons playing in the snow. I scrolled through them, smiling.

Refocusing on my objective to block Cindy, I explored the icons on Joe's home page and clicked around the site. An empty message box opened. I tapped on the word "Archived," curious to see where the tab might lead. I found two messages in the folder and opened them. The first was from a woman I didn't know. The content suggested Joe knew her quite well, maybe even intimately.

What is going on? Why is Joe writing to another woman this way?

I clicked on the second message and found similar writings that included words of endearment. Looking at the dates I realized both conversations took place over a year ago, before Joe even met Cindy.

I exploded.

I shot from the table, grabbed my keys, and ran to my car. My hands trembled. I couldn't get the key into the ignition. I needed to get to Joe's office immediately. If he intended to delete the messages from those two women, there must be more. If I caught him unaware, I could check his office computer, a computer he never expected me to see. The lies were making me crazy. I couldn't trust anything he said. I had to figure it out for myself. I needed to know everything, or I would go insane.

Like that first awful night in December, I screamed as I drove. The messages on Facebook transported me back in time. Now, instead of running away from Joe, I ran toward him, determined to ferret out the rest of the lies. I screamed and yelled and beat on my steering wheel as I raced toward his office.

When my tirade quieted, I turned the car around and drove back to the house. Going to Joe's office would not bring clarity. It would just make me look like a crazy woman.

When I got home, I called him. In a tight, controlled voice I said, "Come home and pack your stuff."

"I don't understand."

"Does the name Tina sound familiar?"

I heard him gasp. "I'm on my way."

When Joe came into the bedroom, my anger was evident but under control. I quietly told him what I'd read on Facebook.

He offered a lame defense. "It was nothing. I didn't do anything. We were just friends."

Joe knew it was a lost cause.

He gave in to my toneless insistence that none of it was okay. "You're right," he said. "I'm sorry."

Joe did not pack his bags. He did not leave.

We have talked about that day, and neither of us remember much beyond his admission that his communications with these women were inappropriate for a married man. He does remember that he almost threw up at his desk when I called and referred to Tina by name. He also said he would have felt better if I had yelled.

My controlled words made it impossible for him to distract me with a return volley of anger. It forced him to admit his intentions regarding these women—and to suffer the full brunt of his shame.

Through our discussions over the next few days, which included a litany of questions and pleadings for the truth, we shed light on an undercurrent of betrayal that spanned eight years of our twelve-year marriage. Joe had been leading a double life for years.

Wednesday, January 30, 2014

I can't stand this. My box is overflowing with the ugliness and lies. The lid won't close, so now I have moved it all to a dumpster. A dumpster full of betrayal. Joe's been having relationships with other women for years. Cindy is only a culmination of years of online and phone encounters.

Now I am the one leading the double life. I am happy to have Joe's full attention. I support him as he resists the temptation to contact Cindy. How crazy is that? And then there's the broken, hidden me that has been betrayed on so many levels. How do I let myself even feel that pain?

I do feel something. I feel like a doormat.

I tried to make Joe understand that his inappropriate interactions with other women were all affairs on some level. He was a mess after our talk, totally defeated. Somehow, he had convinced himself that these "friendships" were okay. Now he knows that his affair with Cindy was just the outcome of a much bigger problem.

I'm afraid he won't be able to stop. He has been cheating on me for years and thought it was okay.

Up to this point my fear and obsession over Joe, his phone, and his computer focused on his interactions with Cindy. Now, the world of what I didn't know about Joe seemed endless. I lived in a war zone, and my only chance for survival was to ferret out the enemy who could be anywhere. I wasn't safe. My insides quivered with fear. My technology skills leapt from novice to expert, using google searches to learn everything I needed to uncover things Joe intended to hide.

Deleted material exposed truth, but so did text messages and Facebook chats. With the camouflage of my ignorance removed, conversations that appeared innocent at first glance revealed inappropriate content and lengthy exchanges, often during work hours.

In some conversations I got the sense that the women loved Joe. In others, flirtation hinted at the thrill of a sexual undercurrent. How did this go on for so long without me knowing? I had been a fool not to see the battle raging all around me. I made it easy. I had a childlike innocence and trusted my husband. Now I was aware of the battle and I lived in fear.

Sunday, February 9, 2014
We have a joint Facebook account now. Last night we got a message from an old neighborhood friend of Joe's. She wrote, "I'm happy to see you and your wife together on Facebook." Later, she texted Joe privately to ask if he was okay. She was looking for him. It makes me jealous. I feel jealous of Joe's female friends. I hate feeling this way. It is painful and feels selfish. I don't want Joe to like anyone but me. I don't want him to have fun with anyone but me. I don't want him to have a life. He says it's understandable, but it is an awful feeling. I wouldn't want to be married to me like this.
I responded to the text from Joe's neighbor for him. I wrote, "My wife and I are doing things differently. I won't be texting anymore." Then I deleted her number.
How did Joe get so turned around?

***

We were driving to the YMCA near our home, chatting, when we figured out where some of it began.

When we first married twelve years ago, Joe worked as an engineer for a mid-sized consulting firm. Two weeks after our wedding, he lost his job. Shocked and humiliated, Joe called to tell me he had been let go.

"It must mean there is something better out there for you," I'd said lightly and meant it.

I hadn't realized how much that job loss hurt Joe. In leaving the company, he also left behind his work buddies. Joe didn't share his shame and loneliness with me, his new bride. He wanted to be my big strong Marine, so he kept his sorrow and self-loathing to himself. It didn't take long for him to find a new job, but his ego had suffered.

Another job loss four years later because of downsizing resulted in an extended period of unemployment. After months of job searching, Joe had difficulty motivating himself to continue the discouraging hunt. He needed a distraction from facing his inadequacies day after day.

One morning Joe checked his email, as he had every day for the last two months, only to find another rejection. Frustrated and bored, he clicked on an instant-messaging site, and for the first time, went into a chat room. Here he found an entire world of distraction, something to take his mind off the laborious task of sending resumes into a void where nothing came of his efforts.

Chatting helped fill the hours surrounding his futile emails. He quickly came across women who made him feel better about himself. The banter was light and entertaining. The admiration became a drug to his bruised ego. Their validation kept him coming back for more. Joe found favorite groups and became a regular.

The chatting seemed harmless until one day, when it didn't. Joe was invited into a private chat, and the friendly banter quickly turned sexual. It wasn't right. He knew he should end the conversation but couldn't seem to break from it. When Joe finally closed the computer, he sat in the dark living room wondering what had just happened.

As we pulled into the YMCA parking lot, Joe said, "I should have come to you when that first chat turned sexual, but I was afraid you would think less of me. I decided to stay quiet and make sure it never happened again."

But it did happen again.

The secret gained momentum and the betrayal grew.

Joe and I were quiet, each trying to fit these revelations into our understanding of the past.

"I can't believe I'm telling you all this," Joe said. "I always wanted to talk to you this way. I was afraid you wouldn't love me if you really knew me." He pulled his keys out of the ignition but made no move to leave the car. "I am so disappointed in myself. When I look in the mirror, I'm not the man I thought I was."

His eyes welled as he stared out the windshield.

"I'll have to live with the mistakes I've made for the rest of my life," he added

I wrestled with my thoughts. I ached to soothe his anguish, but I also wanted him to hurt, believing it somehow eased my own suffering. It didn't. His admissions were painful, but they were his truth, and that's what I had asked for. The truth was that my husband got lost years ago, and now he was trying to find his way back.

I wanted him to make it. I loved Joe too much to let him suffer this alone. I shoved his admissions into the dumpster, reached out, and stroked his arm.

He looked at me. "Thanks, Babe. Thanks for hearing me." Joe turned to open the car door, then stopped. Leaning back in his seat, he said, "I'm gonna be a different man. I want to be a new man—sober, mature, and complete."

The next day, we sat at the kitchen table while a wet February snow fell outside. Joe spoke of his shame and regret over the ways he'd let both of us down. He mourned the time he wasted looking to other women for validation. Joe's self-flagellation reminded me of a time long before we met, when I had been painfully critical of myself. My inner critic had crushed me to a point of hopelessness. A counselor taught me to be my own nurturing parent so I could love the frightened "little Hilarie" inside of me and bring her back to life.

"Joe," I said. "I think there's a little boy inside of you who got scared and lost years ago."

Joe rested his chin on his hand, waiting for me to go on.

I looked at him. "The man in you never left my side. He was an equal, loving partner in our marriage. But you were splintered, and the little boy inside of you didn't feel like he was good enough. The women made him feel better about himself. It's like you were on two paths. Joe, the little boy, went down the path where he chatted with other women. Joe, the man, remained here in our marriage having a good life with me."

He nodded, encouraging me to continue.

"In times of boredom or discomfort your little boy came out, trying to fill holes in his heart that couldn't be filled," I said. "He created a wall of deceit and struggled in secrecy. He didn't want to risk losing me. You led a double life."

I waited.

So did he.

Then I touched Joe's arm lightly. When he looked at me, I held his gaze.

"You need to love that little boy. He needs you to nurture him and make him whole again." My grip on his arm tightened. "Can you picture him, Joe? Do you know who I mean?"

Without a word, he stood and went to the bedroom. I heard him digging through his dresser. A few minutes later he came out, his cheeks wet. He handed me a picture. The little boy was about eight years old with his hair slicked back. He wore a green bowtie.

"That's him," Joe said. "It's me."

***

We live in a small, one-traffic-light town on a two-lane country highway. I work in a school district thirty minutes from our house. Back then, my commute consisted of twenty-two minutes on our little highway and eight minutes getting through town to my school. About a mile from school a set of railroad tracks ran across the road. I'd slow when I approached the slight rise, scan up and down the tracks, then roll over the bumpy rails. The crossing, with its ritualized shift in speed and jostling, became a kind of boundary between my two worlds.

Each morning, I left the house carrying my nightmare with me. While I drove, I tried to piece together a puzzle that was fragmented and incomplete. I often called Joe to continue the round of therapy we'd begun at the breakfast table. Tears were the norm as I struggled with the pain of his honest answers to my relentless questions.

The railroad crossing jolted me into my daytime life, as a teacher for children with special needs. In the busyness of a challenging classroom, I could almost forget the sadness and confusion waiting for me at home. In the afternoon, my car bumped back over the tracks, and I shifted into the nightmare I had left at the crossing that morning. Each time I wondered what more I would learn when I got home.

One afternoon as I drove over the tracks, I lost my fragile grasp on reality. With the jostling, I experienced a powerful surge of confusion. Something in my mind tilted, and I was lost. The landscape of my life became as unrecognizable as a village after a tsunami. Adrift, I floated in a world that wasn't my own.

What am I doing in someone else's life?

My husband's been cheating on me.

No, he hasn't. That's someone else's husband. I'm not her.

A shudder of fear ran through my body.

"I'm not her," I said aloud, my confusion building. "This is someone else's life."

Unable to calm myself, my breathing became shallow. My heart raced. I pumped the brakes erratically, struggling to respond to taillights of the car in front of me.

I need help.

At a red light, I picked up my phone and stared at it. It took a couple of beats to pull my thoughts together. *Call Joe.*

When he answered, I cut off his greeting.

"Talk to me," I pleaded.

"What's wrong?"

"I'm in someone else's life and her husband cheated on her. I'm in the wrong life. I don't know where I am." My breathing came in short pants.

"Are you driving?" he said.

"Yes, talk to me. I'm really confused." I whined like a child. "I just want to go home."

"Pull over, Babe. Find a safe place and stop the car."

"No." I pounded my fist on the steering wheel. "I have to keep going. I'm afraid to stop." I whimpered and panted, my fear escalating.

"Okay, okay. Keep driving and go slow," he soothed. "I'm here. You're okay."

"I don't know where I am." Glancing from one side of the street to the other, I couldn't connect with anything familiar, anything that might quiet the rising panic. "Where am I, Joe?"

"You're all right. I'm here. I'll stay with you. What do you see? Are there any stores?"

He waited.

"I see AutoZone," I said. "And there's a BP. Oh, wait, I remember BP."

"Good. I know where you are. Keep going. Do you see the traffic light?"

"I see it." My breathing came easier. "Okay, I see. I know where I am. I think I do."

We were both quiet.

"Are you at the light yet?" Joe asked.

"Yeah, I'm gonna turn here. I'm good. I'm going home now."

I drove on with the phone pressed to my ear, neither of us talking.

"You still there, Joe?"

"I won't leave you, Babe."
"Okay." I cried softly.
"I'll never leave you."

Chapter 9

Counseling

Clearly, I needed help. I had begun seeing a counselor in late January. When I walked into the old Victorian that had been converted into offices, I was desperate and hopeful. I truly was living in someone else's life. The onslaught of uncontrolled emotion had caused a short-circuit in my mind. I recognized very little about myself or the world that now revolved around Joe and fear. I wished for a connection, a spark of clarity that might help me link my love for Joe, to my new reality.

That first day, the woman who came out of the office introduced herself as Linda. She was a tiny, self-assured woman, her clothing comfortable yet professional. I immediately felt at ease. When I followed her into her office, I smelled something pleasant and noticed lit candles on the low tables.

I sat on the couch she indicated and toyed with the pillow beside me.

"So, tell me what's going on," Linda said.

I eased back into the comfortable cushions. Pulling the pillow into my lap, I took a deep breath and told my story.

Linda was a good listener. She heard my pain and challenged me to move forward. She wanted to focus my energy in a positive direction. On my second visit, she suggested I make a small scrapbook featuring things I loved about Joe. I latched on to her idea like a lifeline.

The next day, I bought a small album and decorated it. I pasted photos into my new love album. I typed up a paragraph for each photo that began, "I love you because…" The book seemed crazy in light of Joe's betrayal, but when I worked on the project it distracted me from my pain.

For weeks, I rode the emotional rollercoaster with my love album. I'd soar high while writing about my love for Joe and our early years together. The ride down the other side was scary and disorienting when images of other women plagued my mind, shredding the positive memories. I'm surprised I didn't take a scissor to my work during a low. I guess I wanted to believe the words of love more than the crazies in my head.

On Valentine's Day, I presented Joe with his gift. The cover of the sage green album had a photo of us kissing. My hand rested gently on top of Joe's ball cap, and he had his arm around my waist.

Joe's eyes misted as he turned to the first page.

"You wonder why I love you," it read. "There are so many reasons. This book is for me, to remind myself of how lucky I am to be married to you, and for you, so you can see the wonderful man that you are."

My words touched Joe. His lip quivered. Watching him, my eyes grew moist, and I sniffled.

The next page held one of my favorite pictures of Joe taken when we first moved into our home together. He wore a bright blue cycling cap with its short bill flipped up. His blue eyes sparkled with joy. Above the picture I had written, "I love you because your laugh makes me smile."

I scooted next to Joe and together we read the book, smiling, laughing, and crying at its contents.

The book reinforced that I really did love Joe despite what he had done. The photos and captions reminded both of us why we married in the first place. The love album gave us a badly needed break from the nightmare. For that one evening we just enjoyed the love we shared.

***

Since the visit with my siblings, thoughts of church had been percolating in the back of my mind. The story about Abram sparked my curiosity. When I talked about it with Angie, one of my classroom aides, she suggested Joe and I try going to her church, Delaware Grace.

Joe grew up Catholic and attended Catholic school through high school. He had little experience with other expressions of faith and was resistant to the idea of going to another church.

Thankfully, his desire to help me heal overrode his discomfort, and he agreed to go.

Nervous anticipation fluttered in my chest on the third Sunday in February, when Joe and I drove to Delaware Grace Church. I hoped I might feel something, as I had at the church in New York. We were greeted at the door and again, people were friendly. We sat toward the front of the spacious room. I smiled when I noticed a large wooden cross on the wall behind the stage. So far, so good.

The service opened in a concert-like atmosphere with enthusiastic singers surrounding us. I sang along. Joe did not. When the music ended, a man in his early forties, dressed in jeans and a plaid button-down shirt, walked onto the stage carrying a worn Bible. We were both surprised when he introduced himself as Pastor Frank. He looked like a neighbor, not a pastor.

With an easy laugh, Pastor Frank talked to the people gathered before him as though we were his friends. When he said, "There are no perfect people here," we knew we were in the right place and we'd be back.

We visited Delaware Grace intermittently while also attending Joe's Catholic church. The music at Grace quieted me, and some of the sermons related directly to our struggles. In one sermon, Pastor Frank said our trials serve a purpose. They help us become mature and complete.

At those words, Joe and I turned to each other, our eyes wide. Hadn't Joe recently told me that's what he wanted? —to become sober, mature, and complete? How did Pastor Frank know?

Church offered a reprieve, but Joe's betrayal and my efforts to hold his attention plagued my thoughts.

Monday, February 17, 2014
How can I ever compete with the unlimited availability of women on the internet? I'm just one person. I will never be enough. I didn't even know it was a competition. I have become hypervigilant. I'm not really sleeping, just dozing, then waking to go over it all again. I have given Joe the power to decide if I am enough. He tells me he feels complete now that he is one person focused on me. I'm all he wants and needs. And I believe him, for now. But what happens later, when the fear of losing me fades?

Joe mentioned yesterday that Cindy's pull is hard to fight. It is difficult for him not to text her. I think that's because of how she made him feel about himself. He got to live out a fantasy. Her attention and the risks brought him a high that can't be replicated in our safe, secure marriage. As wonderful as it is to be rediscovering each other, it won't take the place of his experiences with her. How will he ever think that what we have is good enough?

Okay, I talked to Joe about this. He says the affair had no substance. It was two-dimensional and exciting but not fulfilling. What he has with me is real and complete. I give him more that is solid and lasting. I can't make him feel like she did, but he wants this more.

Regardless of what he chooses, I am enough. I give Joe all I have to give. I can only find peace if I believe I am good enough just the way I am.

***

In late February, sixty-two days after Joe ended his affair with Cindy, he walked into the kitchen and announced, "I've been thinking about something for a couple of days."

He scooted a chair close to mine, then casually said, "I think I need to call Cindy for closure."

My mouth dropped open.

Joe nodded his head, obviously in agreement with himself. "Just a short call to explain what happened. You know, why I ended things so abruptly."

My heart pounded in my chest. "You want to call Cindy."

"Yeah, I still feel tempted to contact her. I think it's because I didn't get to explain things. I just sent her that one text. That's probably why I think about her so much."

He waited for my response. What could I say? I just stared at him, dumbfounded.

"I'm trying to honor our honesty policy," Joe said, an edge of annoyance entering his voice. "That's why I'm telling you."

I wanted to scream. *Are you crazy? You're an idiot! I hate you!*

But I tamped down the fear and the anger that threatened to pour from my mouth. What little influence I might have depended on me staying calm.

I couldn't react, so I tried to reason. "You haven't contacted her since December, right?"

"Yeah, but I want to stop thinking about her, too."

"Meaning you've been able to stand strong since December 23 despite the temptations."

"Right, and this will help support my commitment to you and our marriage." He leaned back. "I wouldn't be doing anything wrong because I'm telling you. No secrets."

"Joe, everything we've read says, 'No contact.'"

"I know, but the intent of the call makes it different. My intent is to get closure."

"Sounds like justification to me," I said quietly.

"Can't you see I'm just trying to fix this? I don't want to be with her. I choose you." He raised his arms then dropped them in his lap. "Anyway, I didn't say I was going to call her. I'm just thinking about it."

I backed off. Maybe Joe's Marine buddy, Ron, could help him see the danger in this. I suggested he give Ron a call.

Joe agreed and left the room.

A rock sat in the pit of my stomach. I couldn't move. Thinking about a phone call to Cindy made me nauseous.

Five minutes later, Joe practically bounced back into the room. "Yeah, I guess you were right. Ron said I shouldn't contact her for any reason. He and I are getting together for lunch on Saturday."

"Good," I managed. *He still doesn't get it.* "I'm gonna go write."

Monday, February 24, 2014

He is relieved and feeling good. What about me? I'm relieved, but what about my sadness? He came so close to calling her. He keeps saying, "I choose you. I choose our marriage." I'm glad he chooses me, but I'm sad that Cindy is still so important. For a couple of days, he has been working up an excuse and making a plan to contact her. He didn't, and that speaks volumes for his commitment, but still, how sad for me. I feel sorry for me. I feel like the consolation prize. I am such a waste today.

The truth is that I want to stay married. If he hadn't told me, our marriage might be over.

***

During one of my counseling sessions, Linda gave me a strategy to shift my perspective on Joe's journey. Although I knew his truth-telling was positive, the things he shared wounded me. It was painful to hear the truth about his thoughts even when he did make the right choices.

"How do I keep from getting depressed when Joe talks honestly about his struggles?" I'd asked.

"From your perspective, everything is the same betrayal," Linda said. "You lump it all into one category. You need to place each truth on a continuum so you can distinguish the positive from the ugly."

"I have no idea what you're talking about. How's that for honesty?"

"Very funny." She went to the dry erase board on the wall, drew a horizontal line, and wrote the numbers one through ten below the line. "This is your continuum."

Above the number one, she wrote, "Affair." Above the number ten, she wrote, "Remorse."

"One is ugly," she said. "Ten is positive. On this continuum, where would you place Joe's honesty about the phone call he *didn't* make?"

"I guess I could give it a seven or eight. Oh, I get it. This will help."

"Just focus on the present with this. Don't go back and try to rate the past. Keep the dumpster closed and stop asking questions. You already know too much."

Tuesday, March 4, 2014

I've told Joe many times how much I hate his phone for the part it played in the deceit. Today I made peace with it. I am trying to look at his phone as a tool to our healing rather than part of our destruction. He says the phone didn't cause this.

I realize that the phone has made a huge difference on this end of things. On December 23, the phone let me know we had a problem. The phone gave me enough information to confront Joe with no doubts. Joe's openness with his phone has helped rebuild some trust. The phone has kept us connected. We have our early morning calls on the way to work. We send love messages and comfort with our texts. I can check in when I feel squirrely. We've also had some good therapy by phone. I use the phone to let Joe know when I am in distress or lost. Occasionally, we have traded phones to give me peace of mind.

So, the phone has been a support for me in this hard job of healing. We couldn't have gotten this far without that connection.

***

On March 10, Joe lost his job.

"The boss dredged up some old rule about no personal use of the internet during work hours," Joe said. "They told me I had the option to resign or be fired. I had no choice. I resigned, but I'll still get unemployment."

Joe suggested that it might be better if he not look for work right away since school would be out at the end of May. He wanted to spend the summer together. I agreed.

I had little emotion regarding Joe's job loss. With everything else going on, I didn't care. I threw it in the dumpster with everything else. At least he wouldn't work in Cindy's town anymore. I felt safer knowing he would be at home.

***

Friday, March 19, 2014

Everything feels different and it's exhausting. I live in the same house and go to the same job. I'm even married to the same man, but nothing feels the same. I have no interest in school, hobbies, or our home. I am obsessed with Joe, and the minute I walk away from him, my world starts spinning.

Time has become distorted. Every minute is full. My emotional swings and our discussions are time and energy consuming and often leave me wiped out. Sometimes I am "in love" with this big strong, man who makes me feel like a cherished woman. And then I remember I wasn't good enough and I feel like Alice in the looking glass where nothing is as it seems.

Joe thinks our communication is better than ever because in the past he couldn't talk to me. I'm glad he feels that way, but I'm Alice—I thought we already had good communication.

I tried to talk to Linda about it and left the counseling session feeling so awful I howled all the way home. She wanted to know why Joe wasn't able to talk to me in the past. She wonders why he needed the distraction of other women. What he got from them that he couldn't get from me. She thinks maybe I intimidate him.

My therapist, who is supposed to be on my side, is making me feel like it's my fault. She said I need to dress the way Joe wants me to. I need to "change things up" in the bedroom. I need to be careful how I talk to him. In other words, I need to stop being me. The fact that I'm going crazy doesn't seem to concern her at all, as long as I check in with Joe to see how HE's feeling.

Maybe it's time to stop going to counseling.

I didn't stop going to counseling. I brought Joe to my next session. He expressed remorse for the pain he caused me. He took full responsibility for his sexual betrayal and validated the trauma that had ravaged my world. Linda saw for herself that Joe was not intimidated by me.

Her suggestions were often helpful, but sometimes she made things worse. Linda focused on moving forward and the things I needed to change about myself. She never addressed my traumatization. In the two and a half months since my initial discovery, I'd been bombarded with painful information. Each time I learned something new, I moved deeper into isolation. Alone in my sorrow, I had no one to confide in but Joe, and it made me crazy. I needed to grieve. I needed Linda to validate my losses and the misery Joe's infidelity caused. I wanted my counselor to hear my pain and tell me it wasn't my fault.

I asked Linda why she wouldn't let me just cry.

She said, "That's not why we're here. We're here to move you forward."

Linda didn't realize that ignoring my pain held me back.

Thankfully, Joe understood. He was all I had.

When we got home from the session, I curled up beside him on the loveseat in our bedroom.

"Joe, I'm so confused. I feel like Alice in Wonderland, where nothing is as it seems."

He wrapped his arm around me. "This is real, Babe. Things are as they seem, now."

"What about before?"

"They weren't," Joe said, resting his head on mine. "I was deceiving you."

"I keep thinking if I work hard enough it will all go away."

"It won't go away. I betrayed you. I can't change that. I'm so sorry I hurt you."

"I'm exhausted," I said.

"I know." He rubbed my shoulder.

"I think I'm going crazy."

"You're okay." He pulled me closer. "You're gonna be okay."

Joe did everything he could, but he couldn't make me feel safe. I needed something more.

Saturday, March 22, 2014

What do I need to do to feel safe? I keep coming back to that. When I'm afraid or sad, I keep turning to Joe. It is scary to go to my abuser for comfort.

This morning I was reading Beyond Codependency *by Melody Beattie and realized I need to put my trust in my higher power. When I'm feeling sad or insecure, I can hand things over to God. I can trust God to keep me safe.*

When Joe shares the truth about his feelings and I don't like the way it makes me feel, I can turn it over to God. I know Joe's sharing is helping us have a better marriage. I'm grateful he loves me enough to risk sharing. Each time he tells the difficult truth, he is investing in our relationship. We are brought closer when he is honest about his actions and feelings.

The truth has the power to rebuild my trust, and the information he shares will only hurt me if I let it. This will work much better if I can turn the hard stuff over to God.

Chapter 10

Disclosure

Continuing to struggle on my own, with no one to confide in, I looked to books for answers. One night in late March, three months after discovery, I spent the better part of a night reading *Not Just Friends* by Shirley Glass. One section caught my attention with these words, "As long as the affair has secrets, the couple cannot heal." Reading through the passages that followed, I rewrote her words in my mind, conforming them to my need. *He has to tell me everything.*

I've gone back and reread Glass's words on disclosure. She cautions strongly against receiving detailed information that might fuel obsession or cause retraumatization. The warnings and structure for thoughtful disclosure are very clear, but on that night in late March, my desire for uncensored truth overpowered all cautionary words. The thought of a single undisclosed detail terrified me. The secrets and lies loomed large and turned me into an isolated crazy woman driven by fear of the unknown. Safety was my primary objective. I convinced myself that hearing every aspect of Joe's betrayal would ensure that it never happened again. I believed that knowing everything would keep me safe and help me piece my world back together.

Morning dawned and Joe had barely opened his eyes when I handed him the book and asked him to read what I'd found. Ever present to my needs, he put on his glasses and read.

When Joe looked up, his eyes told me he understood I needed more information. I was relieved. This disclosure would move us forward.

He took off his glasses. "Are you sure?"

I nodded. "Can we do it right now?" I pleaded.

He squinted at the clock. "You have to get ready for school. We can talk when you get home."

"I was up all night. I already arranged for a sub. I want to talk now."

He rubbed a hand over his chin and pulled on the hairs of the beard he'd grown back. "I won't be able to look at you. I'm so ashamed."

"I know. It's okay. Just tell me everything, so I can understand and put it all in the dumpster."

Joe adjusted his head on the pillow. I sat cross-legged on my side of the bed and pulled a pillow into my lap. A rush of adrenaline swept through me, simultaneously alerting my focus and numbing my emotions.

Gazing at the ceiling, Joe spoke softly. "The whole thing is so big. I don't know where to begin."

"You should probably start with meeting Cindy." My stomach clenched in anticipation.

"Yeah, I guess so." He took a deep breath and blew out.

"When I first met her, I thought she was cute..."

I didn't move, silently willing him to continue.

"We were at run club. Bob introduced us. The three of us started the run together. We left Bob after the first mile. It was fun—I could tell she liked me. I was attracted to her. I saw her every chance I got after that."

I wanted Joe to unburden his secrets, and he did. I settled in and listened, surprised that I didn't have to ask questions this time. He paused often, gathered his thoughts, then shared more of his story.

Looking back, I realize that my efforts to love Joe despite his betrayal made him feel safe. My love enabled him to be vulnerable with me. His willingness to give the information I asked for helped me learn to trust him again. The truth hurt, but eventually it would heal us. Truth was the key to closing the lid on the dumpster.

That day Joe told his story his way. He told the tale of a man who got caught in a sexual experience that made him feel young and desired. His relationship with Cindy washed away the burdensome years of self-doubt. A few harmless lies to me and he was living the dream. But each time, the fun was short-lived, and Joe's heart was heavy with shame and guilt. Still, he answered the call of his flesh and saw Cindy when he could.

Some things I can't remember, and others I will never forget. A flood of details flowed into my memory. Later, the details would become triggers, where seemingly unrelated situations, people, gestures, or objects could ignite panic as I revisited the horrors of Joe's betrayal.

The telling took the better part of the day. During one break I brought out nail polish and did my nails. I had read that self-care was important. I sat at the table in the sunroom, stroking light pink polish onto my nails, my mind numb from the onslaught of unbearable information. At another break, we tried to eat lunch. Joe wolfed down his sandwich in an effort to feed his discomfort, while I poked at mine, my stomach nervous and skittery.

Disclosure was necessary, but this massive dumping of information should have taken place with another man, a trusted accountability partner. I was wrong about the details. They did not bring me peace.

By mid-afternoon, we were wiped out. Joe finished his story, and we lay together on the sunroom futon reading. Both of us fell asleep. When we woke, he appeared relaxed, lighter for having unburdened himself. The weight of his secrets now lay on me. Joe held me close and I cried.

The telling was over. Now, I would gather the images his words created and piece them together in an attempt to clarify my understanding of the past year.

When I was finished sifting through the nightmare, I hoped to shovel the whole mess into the dumpster and be done with it.

Thursday, March 27, 2014

In Beyond Codependency, *Beattie says we don't have to take another person's behavior so personally. I shouldn't take Joe's affair so personally. The behavior was a result of his insecurity, his losing touch with his own values, and his skewed sense of what is and is not okay in a marriage.*

Joe missed out. I was happy living by my values with a man I loved. The fact that he couldn't do the same is very sad for him. Our marriage could have been better for Joe, but I liked it just the way it was. He didn't ruin my part. Joe cheated himself out of a good marriage. It's only in the telling that I get hurt. He's been hurting for years.

The truth about my life today is that I am married to a handsome, fit man who loves me like no one else. He is committed to doing whatever it takes to make me feel safe in his love. He listens to my fears and insecurities in a way that makes me feel heard and validated.

With the new year, we have been able to create a little cocoon where the world revolves around us. We have very few distractions or interruptions as we work to understand and grieve this crisis that has come to light in our marriage. I thought the grieving was predominantly mine. Now, I realize we are both injured and we both need this time together. We are working to rebuild the trust and honesty we lost for reasons neither of us can fully understand. Each time we venture out of our cocoon, I feel relief to run back to life with just the two of us. I'm afraid to tip our delicate balance. I've gone a little crazy and it's scary. We are fragile.

***

On the evening of April 3, Joe strutted into the kitchen and announced, "Today I've been sober for 100 days." He kissed me on the top of my head and went to the cupboard to get a glass.

My forced smile held no joy. *That's great for him, but it means I have been a crazy woman for 100 days.*

My plan to move through the process quickly wasn't going well. I needed to stop looking to Joe for answers. He seemed more confused than I. He claimed our marriage would be better than ever. Sure, better for him. All of it was for him, not me. Better just meant he would stop cheating on me. Great.

I stopped myself. If I wanted to end the feelings of pain over the betrayal, I needed to stop analyzing everything and quit letting my life revolve around events from the past. I didn't do it, I couldn't fix it, and none of it was my fault.

A prayer came to mind that we used to say at a women's Alcoholics Anonymous group I attended years ago, when my life was out of control. As a teenager I had stumbled across alcohol and found it to be a cure for my awkward shyness. In young adulthood, I drank too much and overlooked the impact it had on my life. Later, the pressures of parenting and a divorce escalated my reliance on alcohol.

By the time I turned forty, drinking was my coping strategy, and my life had become unmanageable. I began attending twelve-step meetings and eventually broke from my alcohol addiction. Before each meeting we prayed the serenity prayer. I remembered the words held wisdom.

That evening, when I brought the salad bowl on the table I said, "Joe, I think we should start saying the serenity prayer before dinner. You probably know it: God grant me the serenity to accept the things I cannot change, the courage to change the things I can and the wisdom to know the difference."

"Works for me," he said.

We sat at the table and Joe took my hand. We prayed the first line together: "God, grant me the serenity to accept the things I cannot change."

I stopped. My eyes burned, and I struggled to hold back tears.

"Saying it together is hard," I said. "I don't want to accept any of this."

"I know, but I don't think you'll get better until you do. We can't change it."

"If I accept the nightmare, it feels like I'm saying it was all okay."

"No, Babe. It means you want our marriage more. The prayer says. 'God, grant me the serenity.' Let's make it about us. 'God, grant *us* the serenity.'"

"Okay."

Joe squeezed my hand. "Hey, we can also include turning it over to God, 'accept and turn over.'"

"That does help. He knows none of this was right."

We began the prayer again. "God, grant us the serenity to accept and turn over the things we cannot change."

I smiled. "The courage to change—"

"And celebrate," Joe added.

"All right."

"The courage to change and celebrate the things we can. And the wisdom to know the difference." Joe kissed my forehead. "I like it."

We've prayed our version of the serenity prayer at every meal since that day. As we became more comfortable praying together, we added prayers of gratitude for the gifts of each day and words asking for protection over our battle. We've learned to pray for our children, too, that the Lord may find them, comfort them, and lead them as He has done for us.

***

Later that week, my classroom assistant, Angie, pulled me aside once the kids were gone for the day.

"I think you should know Leslie's been complaining," Angie said.

Leslie, my second classroom assistant, had taken on some of my smaller tasks because I didn't have the energy to do all that was required to run our room.

"Why, what's going on?" I said.

"It's about you. She said she's tired of doing your job."

Embarrassed and annoyed, I didn't know what to say.

"I know things are tough for you right now," Angie said, "but Leslie thinks she is running the whole room. I thought you should know."

"Thanks for telling me. I'll fix it."

"Okay. See you tomorrow."

I waited until Angie closed the door, then put my head on the desk and wept. I thought Leslie was my friend and that we had grown closer since all of this happened. Just yesterday I told her how grateful I was to have her support. Why did she offer to help me if she didn't want to? I felt betrayed. It hurt to realize I couldn't trust her.

The conversation with Angie was the motivation I needed. It was time to get my act back together in the classroom. I went to my supply cabinet and pulled some activities from the shelf. Tomorrow would be a new beginning.

The next day, Leslie appeared confused when I stood at the front of the classroom with a new lesson up on the board. I directed her and Angie to support student participation while I led the activity. The children laughed and clapped as each one took a turn manipulating the materials I provided. Being back in control energized me.

Leslie sat beside one student, intent on their work together. I wondered if she was happy to have me back in teacher mode. I glanced at Angie helping another student back to his seat. She smiled and gave me a thumbs-up.

Tuesday, April 15, 2014

I'm feeling good today. I'm turning things around at school, thanks to Angie. On the way home, I started the usual nosedive with my feelings. This time I handled it differently. I took control of my thoughts. The truth about my life today is that I am a strong woman. I am energetic and healthy. I'm a good thinker and a good person. I'm going to be okay. I'm going to figure this out.

A month later, I lay in bed waiting for my alarm to go off. Sunlight peeked around the edges of the blinds. In two more weeks school would be out, and Joe and I would have the whole summer to bond and heal. I looked forward to being together and getting outside more.

Thoughts of being outside brought triathlons to mind, triggering unpleasant associations. The happiness of moments ago vanished and my thoughts darkened. I felt myself climbing up onto the edge of my dumpster. I perched, ready to dive in and wade through the ugliness.

No! I will not start my day this way.

I lowered myself back to the ground. My efforts to avoid the negativity of the dumpster reminded me of a poem by Portia Nelson, "Autobiography in Five Short Chapters."

In the poem, Nelson repeatedly found herself walking down a street that had a big hole in the sidewalk. Each time she got close she fell into the hole. By the fifth chapter, Nelson realizes it's time to go down a different street.

That poem described my situation perfectly. Back in December, I was shoved into the dumpster when I read the messages on Joe's cell phone. I couldn't get out. I lay there lost and hopeless, covered in the mess.

Even though it was now May, I continued to walk down that same street. I'd stand beside the dumpster with a smile pasted on my face and at the slightest provocation I'd dive right in. Each time, I hoped the situation would become clearer, look different, or even better—not have happened at all. But the truth never changed, and the images I created from the debris remained painful.

Enough. I needed to stop, close the lid and walk away, or even better—walk down a different street.

Chapter 11

Searching for Peace

The cheerful daffodils in the vase beside the sink made me smile. I put sandwiches and drinks on a tray. Now mid-May, it was warm enough to eat on the back deck.

Joe followed me outside carrying *The Shack* by William P. Young, a book he'd been unable to put down. "Jesus and Mack are walking on the water," Joe said. "Jesus is laughing at Mack's soaking wet socks and shoes. He says, 'We usually take them off before we walk on the water.' They're cracking up. It's like their friends." Joe seemed surprised.

"Uh, yeah," I said. "I thought God was supposed to be your friend."

He scratched his head. "I didn't know that."

Joe told me he always thought of God as the Wizard of Oz with fire and smoke. If you made the great and powerful God angry, the consequence was eternity in hell. As a little boy, he believed he could never measure up to God's standards which were also his Mom's. She wanted him to be a "good" Catholic boy, and "number one" among his classmates. Joe never felt like anything he did was good enough.

The thought of making God or Mom angry was scary for the little boy with the green bowtie. Survival meant keeping track of all the dos and don'ts. At a young age, Joe learned the best way to please Mom was to tell her what she wanted to hear. With practice, he became an accomplished liar.

Joe's interactions with God throughout his life consisted only of formal, memorized, recitations of prayer. He had been taught that only priests spoke directly with the Almighty

But now, as a new man, attending a new church, the concept of a personal relationship with God appealed to Joe. Maybe he and God could even be friends.

Joe swung his arms wildly, reenacting Mack's efforts to walk on water. I'd rarely seen his easy smile these past five months, and I missed it. I sat back, enjoying this man who used to make me laugh. For this one moment, sitting on the back deck, I had my best friend back, and we laughed together and talked about God being our friend.

Thursday, May 15, 2014

Now that I'm less needy, Joe can look at his own stuff. He's sad to acknowledge his betrayal. He realizes that when he was broken, he couldn't feel me loving him. The fact that I didn't abandon Joe with all he has shared shows him my love is real.

Joe and I are reading The Shack, *and I can see it changing him. He sees God and his relationship with God in a new light.*

I read that grace rarely makes sense to those looking in from the outside. At times my acceptance of Joe's betrayal doesn't make any sense, but when I'm curled up in his arms, and he comforts me in my pain, it all makes sense. I also read that since most of our hurts come through relationships, so will our healing. Our healing is coming because we have stayed together. If I had run away, I don't know where I would be now.

I will see the gifts in our struggles if I am patient. I already do on good days. It's time to stop beating myself up for being on the receiving end of the nightmare. This is Joe's growth lesson, not mine. I'm just lucky he is willing to do the difficult work of healing.

Thank God we have the resources to give him this time away from work. Even if we totally deplete our savings, it will have been worth it for him to have this healing time.

***

The next day, we joined Joe's youngest son, Brendan, at an outdoor jazz concert in Columbus to celebrate Brendan's twenty-sixth birthday.

The man at the entrance checked my bag, then directed us through the gate. Vendors lined the narrow, open courtyard. Beer booths outnumbered the food booths by a wide margin.

I hadn't drunk alcohol in over twenty years. My drinking days and time spent in Alcoholics Anonymous were a distant memory. But in my darker moments over the past few months, I longed for alcohol's mind-numbing warmth. The emotional rollercoaster had battered at my sobriety. Fortunately, my fear of the addiction was a powerful deterrent. With loud jazz music bouncing off the surrounding buildings and the festive energy, alcohol was a non-issue for me.

We moved through the congested area to a grass-covered hill facing the stage. Halfway up the hill, we spread our blankets on the grass. I stretched out, put my hands behind my head, and watched the clouds drift, while Joe and Brendan discussed a recent ball game.

After a time, Brendan announced he was thirsty and offered to get the first round of beer for the two of them. When he left, I sat up and scooted closer to Joe. We quietly watched the crowd like we always did at events like this. The area in front of us filled with people, and I mindlessly watched them stake out their piece of lawn.

A tan, blonde woman made her way across the area near the stage. Her short white dress stood out in the sea of colors around her. She appeared youthful, athletic, and carefree. I watched her move slowly across the lawn.

I glanced at Joe. He wore sunglasses. I couldn't see his eyes, but it seemed that his gaze followed her.

I swatted his arm. "You're watching that woman in the white dress, aren't you?"

"What woman?" Joe scanned the crowd. "No, I don't know who you mean."

The woman stopped to talk with people sitting on the ground. I pointed. "The woman in the white dress walking in front of the stage." As I spoke, she sat, and I could no longer see her. "I know you were watching her. I saw you."

"No, I wasn't, Babe. I'm not letting my eyes linger on anyone who might be a problem for me."

I didn't respond. Joe reached over and gently rubbed my back. I pulled my knees up and wrapped my arms around them, hugging myself. I observed the crowd more intently. People milled everywhere. No one was content to sit still. Many laughed and carried food and large plastic cups of beer. I noticed women everywhere.

Many of the younger women didn't appear to realize it would be cool when the sun went down. I wore a T-shirt and yoga pants with a sweatshirt tied around my waist. Some of the young women wore short shorts and camis with heeled sandals. Others wore tiny dresses. My heart raced. The pulsing in my ears muffled the voices around me. I trembled.

There are young sexy women everywhere.

"Joe," I said. "When we went to places like this before, you looked at other women, didn't you?"

He nodded once. "I didn't know. I'm sorry. I didn't know it was wrong." He reached to put his arm around my shoulder.

I ducked away. "You thought about sex with other women even when I was right there with you."

Brendan appeared carrying two large cups. "Hey guys, what's up? They only had Budweiser, Dad." He walked to the far side of the blanket, handed a cup to Joe, and sat.

I rolled to my stomach and put my head on my arms. Excruciating pain set in. I thought back to all the times we had been out together at races, parties, the beach, on our ten-year anniversary cruise...

The list was endless.

I rewrote the past through the lens of this latest insight. Every event that once brought me joy suddenly lay in ruin.

Lying on a blanket in the middle of that concert field, I cried silently. I cried while strangers around me drank and laughed, seemingly without a care. They didn't live with a cheater. They didn't know about lies. Loneliness consumed me. They laughed, and a part of me died.

Brendan brought up another ball game and Joe listened, gently stroking my back. I knew he wanted to offer comfort, but we were celebrating a birthday, and the birthday boy was unaware that my perfect life had become a nightmare.

I stood, my face turned away from Joe and Brendan. "I'm going to wander around," I managed.

I walked up the slope away from the woman in the white dress and the short shorts of the others. The top of the hill leveled off and held more vendors. Now, all I saw were beer booths and the pretty women standing in front of them.

I moved through the crowd becoming more agitated. I decided to head downhill toward the entrance. Approaching the narrow courtyard, the smell of beer wafted toward me. The desire to drink pulled, and beer was available. Foaming red plastic cups surrounded me with their malty scent of relief.

Tears trickled down my cheeks. I wanted to stop the pain and knew a drink would do that.

After a brief hesitation, I gave in and reached a hand toward my back pocket to get my wallet.

"Ohhhh," I moaned.

Yoga pants. I wore yoga pants. I didn't have a back pocket. I didn't have any money. I couldn't buy the peace those plastic cups promised. I couldn't numb the pain.

God made me wear yoga pants.

I ran to the nearby ladies' room, went into a stall, and sobbed. Relief? Sorrow? Fear? I don't know. I just cried. An aching mix of emotion tore at my heart and my mind. I wanted to run away from the agony, but with no way to stop the pain, I just had to feel it.

In retrospect, my perception of Joe's wandering eyes was an extreme inflation of reality. In truth, Joe's eyes and thoughts had wandered on occasion, but for the largest percentage of our time together, he was present and focused on me.

Over time, joy returned to many of my memories. Circumstances led us to be intentional about looking through old pictures and discussing past celebrations and events. We deleted some photos and agreed that an event or two belonged in the dumpster. The challenge of reviewing the past was worth it. We resurrected many of our joyful memories.

***

That spring, I searched desperately for something to quiet the fear, something to bring me peace. I knew using alcohol to deaden the pain would have led me further into brokenness, and I was glad I'd been stopped from going down that path, but I needed something.

I had received a meditation CD at Christmas. I liked the lilting music intermingled with the sound of gurgling water and chirping birds. The melody did not drown out the thoughts that battled in my mind, but somehow it softened them. When I downloaded the CD onto my iPod and put in the earbuds that first time, I was hooked. I rarely went anywhere without my meditation music. The melody and birds in my head became one of my many coping mechanisms.

My search for balance continued when Joe and I walked into a small shop one Saturday. The room was lined with tables full of stones. On closer inspection, I noticed many were sorted into tiny labeled boxes. I bent and read one of the labels, "Soothing peace." Another read, "Energizing clarity." I was intrigued and asked why the stones were labeled that way. Following the shopkeeper's explanation of healing crystals, I left the shop with a bag of gemstones that promised to bring me the peace and balance I longed for.

I bought a book and learned all I could about the healing power of crystals. Each morning I carefully chose a combination of stones hoping they would get me through the day. When I felt anxious, I'd reach into my pocket to rub the smooth gems, rolling them over each other with a soft click clack.

The crystals did not bring the peace or clarity I sought. The gemstones gave me something to do with my agitated fingers—nothing else.

One afternoon, I sat in Linda's counseling office, and she picked up a large stack of photos.

"You need to change the voices in your head," she said, flipping through her stack. The photos were mini posters of positive words and quotes.

"How about some happiness?" she said, and handed me a photo card that read, "Happiness is an inside job." A smiley face in the lower corner made me grin.

"Or what about this one?" She handed me a bright green card that said "Choose Joy" in bold letters.

When she offered me a third card, I said, "How do you make these?"

That evening, determined to turn my life around, I scanned the internet for positive quotes:

Look for joy in the journey.

Life is so much better when you focus on what truly matters.
You are good enough.
Find gratitude and you will find happiness.

I believed I'd found my answer. I was going to quote myself into health. For weeks, I spent hours on this project, scanning, downloading, resizing, and sending images out for printing. Each time a package of photos came in the mail, I couldn't contain my excitement. I hung many of the quotes around my bathroom vanity. I bought mini photo albums and carefully arranged the words of hope interspersed with photos of Joe and me. The arrangement was very important. Each picture had to align with the perfect quote.

My little albums became a lifeline to a world where I would one day be joyful and peaceful again. I carried them with me everywhere and slept with them under my pillow.

The positive quote project did fill my time and mind with affirming words, but the power of Joe's betrayal overshadowed much of the possible benefit. The photo cards were just pretty pictures, another effort to distract myself from the nightmare. I continued to obsess over Joe's actions both past and present. I slipped into tears for no apparent reason. I still got confused and lost when I drove. My search for uplifting quotes and photographs was not enough to stabilize a life that had spun out of control.

Five months on the emotional rollercoaster had taken its toll, and the fear brought on by my realization at the concert had tipped the balance. The crazy highs and lows hadn't let up and sleep eluded me.

One night at 2 a.m., I sat at the kitchen table with my laptop waging war with insanity.

Tuesday, May 27, 2014

God, I need help. I'm going crazy. Please help me accept the things I cannot change. I've moved to a different level of fighting reality. The numbness of the initial shock has worn off, and I'm faced with the cold hard facts of Joe's infidelity. I think I'm moving forward and then the full weight of the betrayal slams me in the face again. I can't find a quiet place to put this. Do I have to repeatedly start over each time I move a little further out of denial? I think I'm going crazy.

Our loving was passionate last night, but the passion came from a place of grieving. My murmurings were not the pleasures of intimacy. They were steeped in sorrow. When we finished, I sobbed. So much pain.

Joe said, "The infidelity will never go away." He's right. I will always have shared him with other women. I will always feel like a doormat. Do I want to be married to Joe after all he's done? Can I really heal from this? Do I want a marriage with infidelity as part of our history?

I've been trying to recreate the dream marriage I thought we had. The dream was a lie. I need to get over it. We didn't have a good marriage. We had a shell of a marriage. I just assumed I wanted this marriage. I haven't really considered the alternative.

I don't have to stay with Joe, do I, God?

I feel calmer realizing I have a choice. Leaving would be hard, but why haven't I even considered it? I assumed I was stuck, that I had no choice. I do have a choice. I can choose to walk away. I can take care of myself by starting over. Regardless of the changes Joe makes, if I can't live with what he's done, I don't have to.

I think God just answered my prayer for sanity. I have a choice. I love Joe, but I need to love myself more.

I couldn't wait to tell Joe what I'd figured out. I felt lighter with this new understanding—an awareness that I wasn't stuck. Realizing I could leave the marriage, gave me the hope I desperately needed. God gave me back my power.

As soon as Joe woke, I shared the good news. "I don't have to go crazy, Joe. I can just leave if I can't take any more of this."

I was now the clueless one. In my self-absorbed relief, I didn't realize my enthusiastic declaration that I could leave our marriage added a burden of fear to Joe's fragile promise to be honest.

If he continued to be truthful about his battle, I might leave.

The first day of June dawned warm and sunny, a perfect day for a swim workout. We packed our gear, hopped in the car and headed for the lake. Joe turned up the radio and we sang and laughed together.

"How far are you planning to swim?" I asked when we pulled in the parking lot. I hoped to swim the full length of the beach, down and back, a distance of a half-mile.

"Depends how cold the water is," he joked.

We got out of the car and put on our wet suits, wriggling and pulling to stretch the second skin over our bodies. Joe pulled the tight zipper up my back, and I realized he'd gotten quiet.

I turned to him. "You okay?"

"Yeah, I'm good."

The water called to me, our first open-water swim of the season. I looked forward to feeling the gentle roll as I slipped through the waves. We grabbed our goggles, swim caps, and towels out of the back seat and headed toward the water.

Partway across the sand, Joe stopped and turned to me. "Is being here a trigger for you?"

Joy drained out of the moment. "No," I said. "I guess I kind of forgot."

Joe kicked at the sand and we resumed walking.

Memories from a year ago rushed in: Waving to triathlon friends when they pulled into the parking lot; chattering about upcoming races as everyone squeezed into wetsuits; Joe asking Cindy about a leg injury.

I replayed the day with an overlay of all I had learned. In my reruns, I starred as the fool. We were at the lake with our friends, and Joe was having an affair with one of them.

No. I pushed the thoughts away. *I will not do that to myself. It's over.*

We spread our towels on the ground and put on our swim caps and goggles. Trying to find words that might bring joy back into the moment, I looked at Joe.

In an instant, my anger flared. He wore the swim cap from his big race last November. A cactus logo and Ironman Arizona were printed along one side.

I pointed at the cap. "Now, that's a trigger. I feel used when I think about that race."

Joe grabbed the swim cap off his head, threw it on the towel, and strode to the water. He dove in and I followed, hoping the water would cool me down.

I swam hard, my arms pounding the water in anger, my breaths rushed as I turned my head quickly from side to side. I kicked with fury, churning the water behind me.

The exertion was short-lived.

Rolling to my back I gulped for air, then bobbed in the gentle waves like a water-soaked log. I watched the clouds overhead and waited for my breathing to slow. My anger faded.

I hate being angry. I especially hate being angry at Joe. It's scary. I feel out of control.

I continued to bob, quieter now, my breathing settled. *I don't want to be angry anymore.*

I rolled over and resumed swimming.

My strokes flowed in an easy rhythm and I thought about my reaction to the swim cap. Joe's affair wove all through his preparation for Ironman Arizona. Without his race training, there would have been no excuse for all the time he'd spent away from home. He used the time to create a life that revolved around himself and Cindy. In supporting his training, I became an accessory in the deceit and a member of the audience celebrating his accomplishment. The race was a lie.

Joe didn't make it to the far end of the beach. He got out of the water and walked back to the towels. When I joined him, he sat with his arms wrapped around his legs.

"It was all a waste," he said. "If you don't feel good about that race, then all that work was for nothing."

He put his head down on his knees.

Finishing the Ironman had been important to Joe, but I couldn't honor his accomplishment. That was the price for his deception. In my opinion, Ironman Arizona belonged in the dumpster with the rest of the nightmare.

On our way back to the car Joe threw his swim cap in a trash can.

I smiled, just a bit.

***

I looked forward to my early morning writing, my time with God. Our visits often took place between 2 and 4 a.m. When I felt the pull to write, I quietly climbed out of bed and carried my laptop to the kitchen.

One morning in late spring, I put my laptop on the table, pushed open the sliding door, and stepped onto the deck. The crickets in the woods beside our house chirped and twittered noisily. I took a deep breath of the warm moist air and let my shoulders drop. Peaceful. Things inside of me were changing.

I went back in the house, ready for the comfort my writing would bring.

Monday, June 2, 2014
  Good morning God. Thank you for the beautiful morning. I feel more like myself today. I have a bunch of projects going on all at once, just like the olden days. I've been much better since I realized I am not trapped. I am not a victim here. I can choose to stay in our marriage or not. I get to make that choice every day. I have many choices. I can choose to take the gift of this marriage and this husband and make it a good day. I can choose whether to live in the past, which has so much potential to destroy me, or in the present with a man who is now a different person. I can either make myself crazy about Joe's distracted past or be grateful to have his full attention now. He loves me like no one else, and I'd be a fool not to make the most of his love.
  Thank you for the reminder that I have choices, God. Thank you for walking with me and carrying me on this rocky road.
  Yesterday Joe and I talked about eye-bouncing. I read that instead of staring at attractive women, a man is supposed to bounce his eyes away. Joe agreed it was a good idea. Then he said, "I can't believe we are able to talk so openly about this stuff."
  I thought we could have talked like this before, but maybe not. I probably would have made it all about me instead of realizing my husband has a darkness inside that he doesn't want to feed. I have to remember that when he tells me stuff. If I get defensive or upset, he will be less likely to share in the future. I have to be willing to listen and then thank him for sharing.
  It is hard to admit that good things are coming out of the nightmare, but Joe and I are meeting this challenge head on. We are sweeping away the brokenness as it comes to light. We are not afraid to talk and dig into the hidden lessons. Each discussion carries the potential gifts we can receive from the nightmare. We have already learned so much. It is exciting to think there's more.
  In our efforts to love and support each other we have begun to tap into possibilities that have been waiting for us all along. Who knew that the amazing love we have always had for each other could reach even greater heights? Like Joe has said all along, "We will be okay. We will be even better than okay." I love this man so much.

Later that day, I stretched out on the futon in the sunroom. A light breeze cooled the room. Joe sat in a rocker reading his copy of *The Shack* for the second time. I picked up my copy and settled in.

In the story, a young man, Mack, loses his youngest daughter in a fatal kidnapping. The police found evidence of the little girl's horrible death at the shack. Years later, Mack is lost in sorrow over his daughter's death. He receives a note inviting him to return to the shack. The invitation appears to have come from God. Mack answers the summons, but on arrival, his pain is unbearable, and we fear he will commit suicide.

"That's how I felt at Christmas," Joe said.

"What?" I sat up, surprised.

"I wanted to kill myself."

Joe lay the book on the table and explained.

Last Christmas, when I'd looked at his phone, Joe's two worlds collided. Cindy was no longer locked up tight in a secret world of anticipation, risk, and sex. The wall Joe had built between life as my loving husband and the excitement of his affair crumbled.

He recalled driving home from New Jersey in total silence. In his stupor, he was unable to imagine the next step. When he got home, Brendan and Kelley were waiting to celebrate Christmas. They opened gifts together, but Joe couldn't make it special. He wanted to be alone.

"When Kelley and Brendan left," Joe said, "the house got so quiet."

He slowed his rocker. "I walked in the bedroom and broke down crying. The room felt empty without you there."

I hadn't thought much about Joe's state of mind at that time.

He moved across the room and sat beside me on the futon. I put my arm around him.

"I knew I had to tell you I'd slept with her. If I kept it to myself, our marriage would have died a slow death. The thought of telling you and then losing you was unbearable. I wanted to walk out in the street and step in front of the next truck."

"What kept you from doing it?" I waited, watching as he searched for a response.

"It was something you said before you left with Emily. You told me I better not get in an accident on the way home." He smiled. "It gave me hope."

Chapter 12

The Nightmare is Over

Friday, June 27, 2014
It is time to close the lid on the dumpster. I keep pulling out old stuff and bringing the ugliness into our new marriage. Each time I do that, I invite the rotting stink of the nightmare to foul up another moment of our life. When I bring up Joe's past behavior, I recreate something that's gone. The thoughts are painful for me and embarrassing for Joe. I ruin what is by reminding myself of what was. The past brought us the gift of right now, but it also has the power to destroy it.

I want to close that dumpster and keep it locked up tight. There is nothing of value there. We have sifted through it with a fine-toothed comb and learned all we can. The nightmare is over. It won't happen again. The horror is too huge for us to risk going back there. I want to slam that lid so hard that the sound will ring in my ears for weeks, reminding me to stay far away from the rot, stink, and pain of its contents. I want to wrap chains around the dumpster and put padlocks on it. I want it to stay sealed up tight forever.

But I have to be realistic. Having the desire to lock it up tight and throw away the key is a step in the process. I may wander near the dumpster. I may even stand close enough to smell the rot. Unfortunately, I might lift the lid. Letting go of pain is a process. Wanting to do it is the first step of the process.

I'll get the padlock on that dumpster one of these days. I just have to be patient with myself.

On July 10, six and half months into our healing, I opened my eyes to bright sunlight. I heard Joe in the kitchen cooking up his specialty, scrambled eggs. Stretching, I looked around our bedroom and realized I felt peaceful, grateful, and excited about my marriage. Happiness settled in. The dumpster sat quietly in the far corner of my mind. I rested, thinking of how far we'd come.

In the winter, we were a mess trying to pick our way through the debris of anger and shame. Every day brought a new contest of survival. I cried, and Joe held me. We didn't know if we would make it. On good days, I remembered I loved Joe and tried to understand him and offer forgiveness. On bad days, Joe stood in the storm of my anger determined to accept the consequence of his choices. He did not defend or shift the blame on to me. He had wounded me and took full responsibility for it.

When spring came, I dabbled with acceptance. My attempts to accept the things we could not change brought hope and helped us move forward. The darkness loomed, but we saw glimmers of something better up ahead.

Then came summer, and I began to recognize some important truths of my own. Life isn't always fair. Sometimes people we love will fail to meet our expectations. I had been focused on my pain and sorrow over all I had lost, the things I didn't know about Joe, and the ways he had hurt me. I'd been angered by his struggles to resist Cindy.

Maybe I needed to get over myself. This wasn't all about me. The discovery, disclosures, and battles with temptation were about Joe's difficult journey out of brokenness. My best friend wanted to get well, and God chose me to help him.

Joe poked his head in the door. "Hey sleepyhead, want some yummy breakfast?"

I jumped out of bed, ran across the room, and wrapped my arms around his neck. "I'm feeling happy today."

"Oh, good." He enveloped me in his arms. "I'm glad." I heard the smile in his voice. "Let's celebrate by having some scrambled eggs."

We finished eating and Joe picked up Melody Beattie's *Language of Letting Go*. The daily meditations were now part of our morning ritual. Joe read the selection titled, "Proving it to Ourselves."

After he read the page, I moaned. "I'm so codependent. I've been trying to prove to *you* that I'm good enough, when *I'm* the one who needs to believe it."

Joe gathered our plates and kissed the top of my head. "I think you're the grand prize, but you're right. You need to believe it." He took our dishes to the kitchen.

I sat staring at the flowers in the middle of the table thinking about my value. The betrayal crushed me because I believed Joe's behavior made me insignificant. I wanted him focused on me so I would have value. My hyper-vigilance was rooted in fear. If I wasn't good enough, he might choose someone else.

Beattie's words reminded me that Joe doesn't get to decide my value. God does. I am good enough just the way I am. I don't have to prove it to anyone. If I could just remember that, the fear might leave me.

***

On August 1, we sat in a small room at Riverside Hospital with Joe's daughter, Kelley, who was recovering from a brief hospital stay. Kelley dozed while Joe and I read.

A small woman carrying a clipboard knocked and entered the room. A tall young man followed her. The woman introduced herself as a physical therapist, and the young man as a student studying to be a physical therapist assistant. She asked Kelley questions about the apartment she lived in and her general functioning at home. "Does your apartment have stairs? How many? Do you use a tub or a shower?" The list went on.

Next, the student asked Kelley to move to the edge of the bed. He wrapped a cloth belt around her waist, explaining that the belt would support her if she got dizzy. Kelley stood when instructed and walked into the hall with the student.

Joe, entranced with the whole interaction, followed them. When they returned, the physical therapist gave her approval for Kelley to go home in the morning.

That evening Joe asked what I thought about him going back to school to be a physical therapist assistant. I liked the idea of Joe doing life differently. A new man needed a new job.

He got on his computer the next day and found a physical therapist assistant program at a local community technical college. By the end of the week, Joe was registered for the prerequisite classes he needed to take before applying to the program the following year.

It wasn't until he started school later that month that I realized he would be spending the next three years on a college campus surrounded by young women. We discussed the dangers of this close proximity to temptation. Joe assured me he would quit the program if being on campus affected his commitment to sobriety. He planned to keep his interactions with female classmates cordial and superficial.

By the time I returned to work that August, Joe and I were doing better, but other important relationships in my life had suffered. I considered my daughters to be friends, but for last seven months I had kept my daily struggles from them. When we spoke on the phone, I lied. I pretended things were fine. My world revolved around fixing my marriage and surviving disclosures and triggers. That didn't leave much for me to talk about.

I shared my concern about my daughters with my assistant, Angie and asked if I should tell them the truth.

Angie didn't hesitate to offer her opinion, and that was a clear, "No." As a teenager, Angie's mother often spoke to her about her father's betrayal. Angie wished she never knew any of it. She remembered her mother's pain, and her relationship with her father suffered because she knew too much.

Angie suggested that I call it "marital challenges" and leave it at that. Relieved, I took her advice and kept my secrets.

***

Driving home from church one Sunday in late August, Joe brought up the sermon topic.

"I was surprised when Pastor Frank said that pride is a sin." Joe maneuvered the car onto the main road.

"I think I might be prideful," I said. "I've always been independent, and I don't feel like I really need other people. Is that what Pastor Frank meant?"

"It might be. Give me an example."

"Well, like at school when I hear teachers chatting in the hall, I don't go out and join them. I feel like they're wasting time. I guess I kind of feel like I'm better than them because I'm working and they're not. That's pretty prideful, huh?"

I didn't wait for him to answer. "Friday was Leslie's birthday. All morning people came into our classroom with good wishes and jokes about her turning sixty. Even though it's my classroom I felt excluded from the fun. I just kept working at my desk. Watching them made me realize how lonely I am. I don't know why I've done that to myself, and I don't know how to change it."

I added, "When I'm at work, other people are like background noise. They're a distraction from my paperwork. When I do talk to them, I'm awkward because I haven't paid attention to things that are important to them."

Joe pulled into the driveway but made no move to get out of the car. "Frank did say we have to take the focus off ourselves."

"I didn't know I was prideful, Joe." My eyes filled. "I hate messing up."

"It's okay. You know now."

"Why are so many things difficult for me?" I asked.

"Frank would say it's because you're human."

"Frank is very annoying," I whined, then laughed at myself.

"Yeah, but he's helping us figure things out."

Nine months after discovery, I still looked forward to a time when my peaceful days would outnumber the crazy ones. Sometimes I forgot about the nightmare for a while and Joe and I would actually laugh together, but those moments were short lived. Most of the time I was in survival mode.

Monday, September 15, 2014

God, help me put it down. I'm so tired of working on this. It's like a gloomy cloud follows me around just waiting for a quiet or weak moment to slip in negative thoughts.

I look forward to the day when I can wake up with no questions. No more trying to reconcile the past. I look forward to a time when I can go for more than a day or two without thinking about Joe's brokenness. I'm so tired. It is like a tornado is swirling on the edge of my consciousness. I'm happy for a bit, but then the tornado catches my eye and the gloom returns. Sometimes when I look at it full on, I can stand strong and not get swept in. Other times, I'm sucked in and the spiraling starts. Even when I'm standing firm, it takes something out of me. Right now, I'm tired from our weekend.

At church, Pastor Frank talked about social media. I hate Facebook and how it took Joe away from me. I think about being part of the church and wonder if I will ever tell people about Joe's infidelity and our recovery. My new friend, Kate, says Joe and I are cute because we hold hands throughout the service. She doesn't know it's because I am afraid.

God, help me to have peace. Help me to live in the moments that are here for me right now. Please help me accept the love that Joe is pouring over me. Help me let go of the negative thoughts that remain so close to the surface. Help me continue to move toward the clear skies that are available to me.

I don't want to live in this dark place giving so much of my energy to something that is out of my control. I'm tired of having to work so hard.

***

The following weekend we made a quick trip to New York for our grandson's ninth birthday. On the way back to Ohio, Joe surprised me by heading east toward the ocean instead of west toward home. I am a beach girl at heart. I spent much of my childhood swimming and playing in the saltwater off both the north and south shores of Long Island, New York. Joe knew an hour or two by the water would revitalize me.

We drove over the bridge onto a six-mile stretch of land at the northern tip of New Jersey's seashore. The salty air smelled like home.

We pulled into the empty parking lot and I jumped out of the car. The overcast, misty day had discouraged other late-season beachgoers, but I took off my shoes and ran over the dunes. Like a little girl, I leapt about on large rocks that lay half buried in the sand and laughed when caught in the spray of waves rolling onto shore.

Joe and I walked up the beach, stopping to pick up shells and colorful pebbles. Seagulls swooped and called, looking for treats. Sandpipers scurried toward the receding water, then made a quick retreat as the next wave bubbled toward them. The mist frizzed my hair and felt wet on my skin. The dampness cleansed me, washing away my worries.

Later, sitting with Joe on the empty beach, the sound of crashing waves and screeching gulls drowned my unwanted thoughts. I wished we could stay forever. When it was time to leave, I walked back to the car dragging my feet. At the top of the dunes, I turned toward the ocean, closed my eyes, and held my arms wide.

Thank you for this day, God, and thank you for this beautiful beach.

We dusted the sand off our legs and feet and climbed into the car. Joe turned the key in the ignition, and I wondered what we might learn today on the nine-hour drive home. Driving time was a prime opportunity for us to discuss books, our marriage, and the changes we were experiencing.

Three hours later, we stopped for a quick lunch. We carried our meal outside and sat at a sunny table beside the parking lot. Joe talked about last week's workout at the Y and mentioned that he'd bought a pack of cookies on his way home.

I looked up in surprise. Joe and I both tend to overeat sugary treats. We agreed to work together on controlling our sugar habit and to be accountable to each other. When I slipped, I told Joe about it. I thought he did the same. That was our deal.

"You bought cookies last week?" Maybe I'd misunderstood.

"Yeah, I messed up on our sugar fast," he said quickly.

"But you promised to tell me the truth in all things," I said.

With a bit of prodding, he admitted he'd bought cookies on several occasions and had neglected to mention it.

I was angry. "Cookies? Really? You have to lie about cookies. I'm not your mother, Joe. I don't care what you eat. If you can't tell the truth about cookies, how will you ever tell me the truth about women?"

I wanted to scream but people were eating nearby. I lowered my voice. "You've been lying by omission our entire marriage."

I couldn't trust Joe. How could he possibly change a lifelong habit of lying? I felt like giving up.

We got in the car and drove in silence, each of us trying to work out the implications of this latest revelation. I couldn't understand why the mess kept getting bigger. I stared blindly out my window and let the numbness seep in.

Joe startled me when he spoke. "I think I've been lying to protect myself from the consequences of telling you the truth. I need to own my truth whether it upsets you or not."

I thought about that for a moment. "It would work better that way," I said. "Then at least I'd know what's going on."

"I'm going to work really hard to be honest with you. If I want to be sober, mature, and complete, that means I have to tell the truth. About everything."

It took a few days to quiet the fears ignited by Joe's lies of omission. When I felt stronger, I wrote this journal entry.

Wednesday, September 22, 2014

The truth about my marriage to Joe is that my expectations have been shattered. But only my expectations. I have not been shattered. I think I will actually come out of this with a stronger sense of self. I am learning to be more comfortable with other people. At school I'm starting to hang out with other women. I feel valued and included. I think I will also learn to value myself more in my marriage. I'm getting stronger.

Today, Joe's professor asked the students, "What is one of the accomplishments that you are most proud of?" Joe told the class he is most proud of the fact that he and I worked together to blend our families. Our seven kids consider each other siblings. It surprised me that he didn't mention Ironman or being a Marine. I love that Joe is trying to redefine who he is and where his priorities lie.

I went for a walk in the woods behind our house after school. While I wandered by the creek, I thought of the question Joe's teacher asked. What accomplishment am I most proud of? The one that stands out for me is the decision I made in 2001, at forty-five years old, to marry Joe and move from New York to Ohio.

I was happy in New York. I took a big risk, leaving everything I knew, everything that was working. It took a leap of faith. After two failed marriages, I chose to try again. I loved Joe so much and trusted he was the right man for me. I wanted to spend my life with him and grow old with him. I risked everything to follow him across the country. I also trusted I would not lose my girls in making this move. I had invested so much love in them over the years. I had to believe the distance wouldn't take them away from me.

Joe and I had a fun wedding in New York, and then I climbed into a U-Haul with my new husband and followed him into our new life.

Our marriage exceeded my expectations in every way. We have been best friends, teammates, partners through the tough stuff, confidants, cheerleaders, and co-parents. I never had reason to doubt him. Never, until earlier this year, did I question that decision.

As 2013 came to a close, I did it again. I took a huge risk, a leap of faith. I let love guide me when I left New Jersey after Christmas and followed Joe back to Ohio. I knew grief awaited me, but I couldn't give up on this man. I couldn't walk away as I had in my past marriages. I believed we would survive the nightmare.

I am proud of myself for being able to endure the horror of those awful early days of confusion and discovery. I am proud of us for meeting the nightmare head-on. We stood in the storm, holding onto each other. We feared the next wave of pain or anger might cause us to lose our grip, washing us into separation and divorce. Joe never left my side, and I never pushed him away. All along he kept saying, "Whatever it takes, Babe," and "We will be okay. We will be better than okay."

I believed him. Even then I trusted him. I wanted him to be right.

Looking back at this journal entry, I am amazed by my courage. In the beginning I wanted to run from the lies and betrayal. At times I thought of myself as a doormat, that only a fool would continue to love her husband after all I had learned. Yet I stayed.

I'm glad I was brave enough to stay.

Chapter 13

God is Here

Tuesday, October 6, 2014
I'm trying to stop the continuous processing. Every little thing can send me into mind games. I have an emptiness inside of me. It's a deep, dark space like a gaping hole. When I stop processing, the emptiness gnaws at me. The hole is there waiting to suck me in. I don't know what filled it before and I don't know how to fill it now. Giving in feels like the only option. I want to be joyful and peaceful, but there is a hole inside of me.

I have pretended it isn't there with my incessant work on our marriage, digging and digging trying to understand. No, maybe it isn't digging. Maybe I'm really shoveling, shoveling as fast as I can trying to fill the hole. I've shoveled in empathy, understanding, acceptance, forgiveness, and sex, but it isn't working. Pouring all of my energy into the hole is not going to fill it. But if I stop, if I just sit still and admit there is a hole, I don't know if I will survive the pain.

I am exhausted. I have no more energy for this. I have to stop. I have to allow the walls of the hole to collapse in on themselves, to become a new normal. It is scary. I don't feel safe because I don't know what is going to happen. I have to be still and let the hole fill back in.

In early October, ten months into our new life, my emotional rollercoaster leveled off. The irrational ride, with its raging dips into sorrow or anger and its peaks of overwhelming love, seemed to have ended. My highs now presented as "okay" and the lows as "melancholy," leaving me feeling flat and dull.

My vigilance over Joe, all the reading and writing, had changed nothing. I used up my energy trying to fix things, and still, the lid on the dumpster remained open. Cindy still visited my thoughts during our most intimate moments. I heard the voices of the other women in my mind late at night. My efforts to close the dumpster failed. The betrayal persisted in taunting me and I just let it. I gave up hoping things might change.

Until one day when I heard a voice inside my head.

It whispered, *You're going to be okay, Baby Girl.*

My spinning thoughts quieted as I puzzled over the source of the words. Was I truly going crazy or had someone called out to me?

Be still and think of me.

Then silence.

Understanding dawned. God was here. I felt Him inside of me, inside my broken heart. Could He fill the emptiness? Would He keep me safe? I didn't know, but His voice brought comfort and for a moment, my thoughts were of Him. Just for that moment.

On Saturday morning, I ran through town listening to an audiobook on my iPod. The combination of warm sun and cool air lifted my spirits. Through my earbuds, Wayne Dyer suggested that we can change our attitude about negative situations in our life by renaming the problem. Our label for a depressing event can keep us stuck and block us from moving forward. Change the label and you change the energy.

I paused my iPod and ran the next two blocks in silence. With my thoughts turned inward, I worked on Dyer's suggestion and saw the wisdom. I had dubbed our situation "The Nightmare." The label referred to anything remotely related to Joe's sexual brokenness. The label helped me to lump it all together, but it didn't help me to stop thinking about it.

If I changed the name to something positive with words that pointed to our growth and healing, it might help. I thought of another name: "Joe's Life Lesson." That had a positive ring and focused on growth and the good choices Joe made.

I turned at the next corner and ran across the train tracks onto a small stretch of road through the cornfield.

Joe's Life Lesson. I smiled and realized my mistake. I couldn't make this all about Joe. The journey was about our marriage, and we were both doing things differently. We had learned a lot this year. "Our Life Lesson" made more sense and put the focus on our healing. We were broken. God found us, and now we were rebuilding our marriage with His help.

I picked up my pace and sprinted the final yards to our house. I couldn't wait to tell Joe my new name for the nightmare.

**

Weeks earlier, a woman at church had handed me a flyer for a Christian women's retreat. The event kept coming to mind. I felt drawn to the retreat for some reason. Maybe God wanted me to go. If I let the weekend pass without attending the retreat, I would always wonder what I had missed by not going.

I decided to go and see what God wanted to show me.

On Friday, October 17, I drove to a facility in a nearby town where the "Touch of God" women's retreat was being held. I signed in at the registration table, put on my name tag, and followed a kind woman into the dorm room. Five sets of bunk beds lined the wall. I hadn't realized I would be sleeping in a room full of strangers. I chose the top bunk in the far corner. A window above the bed provided a view of the woods beside the building. The trees comforted me.

That evening, the speaker said, "God loves us *because* we are sinners. If people were perfect, they wouldn't need God and his forgiveness." Her words validated my decision to forgive Joe. God forgives us when we mess up and He wants us to do the same for others.

Later in the evening I spoke with some of the women. They were surprised I'd come to the retreat by myself without knowing anyone there. I couldn't explain why I was there but believed I would find out before going home the next afternoon.

I slept well in my bunk beside the window and woke ready for whatever the day might bring. After breakfast and worship time, we broke into small groups for discussion. A woman I hadn't seen before rushed into the room at the last minute and sat next to me. The leader opened with prayer, then presented the discussion question. "When is a time that God has touched your life?"

No one spoke so I raised my hand, and everyone turned their attention to me.

"I think God touched my life recently," I said. "My husband and I were going through a really tough time. I felt trapped in hyper-vigilance and fear." My voice trembled. "When I couldn't stand it anymore, I wrote about my craziness and asked God to help me. A little later it seemed like God wrote back. He told me I wasn't trapped, that I had a choice. I could leave my marriage. If I felt too crazy, I could just leave."

I took a sip from my water bottle. "After writing that, I felt alive and hopeful again. I asked God for help, and He gave me my power back. I'm staying in my marriage. I just needed to know I had a choice."

I sat back and blew out a deep breath. These ladies knew about God, and they seemed to believe He had touched me. I looked forward to hearing about the other women's experiences.

A few more ladies shared, then the room grew quiet. The leader shifted her things. I panicked. *No, we can't be done.*

"I want to hear more stories," I blurted.

As if on cue, the woman next to me leaned in. "Okay, I'll tell one."

As she spoke of the struggles in her marriage, I realized she walked in my shoes. Tears welled in my eyes as her words validated my pain. She understood my heartache because she lived with it also.

When she finished, our leader closed the meeting with prayer. During the prayer, I took the hand of the woman next to me and cried openly. Now I knew why God sent me to the retreat. He didn't want me to be alone.

Most of the ladies left the room, but the woman next to me stayed and introduced herself as Cathy. She handed me a box of tissues. "Is he still lying to you?" she asked.

Did I misunderstand her sharing? "No, we're past all that," I said. "Our issue is infidelity."

Nodding, she said, "Mine, too. I love my husband, and he works hard, but when he slips, he lies. He went to the 180 support group at Vineyard Church. It's for guys with sex addiction issues. He said it helped."

I wrote down the name of the church and the men's support program. We exchanged phone numbers and made a date to get together on Monday. Finally, I had someone to talk with, someone who understood.

***

The retreat was just what I needed. Driving home, I laughed. I'd been right about God sending me to the retreat. He wanted me to meet Cathy.

I turned into our empty driveway. A golden-orange carpet of maple leaves spread across the lawn in front of our log home. I felt a rush of gratitude that Joe and I still lived here, together.

I pulled my suitcase up the bumpy sidewalk, past the marigolds blooming in the small garden. In the kitchen, the countertops glistened. A small pumpkin sat beside the stove. I kicked my shoes onto the rug at the back door.

In our bedroom, the smoothed bedspread and vacuumed carpet added to my sense of well-being. Joe had even vacuumed my closet floor. It was good to be home. I put my things away and wandered through the house.

Sun streamed through the skylights, brightening the front hall. I ran my hand along the banister and entered the living room. The baby grand piano filling one corner had rarely been touched since Emily moved out. Maybe this Christmas the kids would all come home, and Emily would play carols for us.

I sat in the swivel chair at Joe's desk beside the piano. Twisting back and forth, I thought about Cathy's question. "Is he still lying to you?"

It saddened me to think of her living with lies. Thankfully, we had shoveled all of Joe's into the dumpster. As a new man, he promised there would be no more lies. The betrayal was over, done, locked up tight in the dumpster.

In fact, I could prove it.

I powered up the computer, opened the web browser and brought up Joe's history. I clicked on the site at the top of the list.

A picture of a woman in sexy underwear filled the screen.

My heart slammed into my chest, and I was transported back to that December night. Fear and anger engulfed me.

Cathy's words rang in my ears.

Yes. Yes, he's still lying. He's lying by omission.

Again.

Shocked, I didn't know what to do. I began clicking through the images.

No. No. Stop.

I exited the site and sat, stunned. Adrenalin flooded my body. My insides trembled.

My husband looks at porn? How could that be? He never mentioned pornography.

I wanted to scream, yell, and jump up and down.

Maybe I should go back to New York. Done. Marriage over.

I turned back to the computer and read through more of his history. Frantic, I scrolled through documents, emails, and images searching for evidence of more betrayal. There had to be more.

I was struck by a sudden wave of clarity and my fingers stilled. Finding more wouldn't erase what I'd already seen.

The trembling stopped. I stood.

Like a sleepwalker, I moved to the sunroom and sat in a rocker. I looked out at the yard. Birds in the feeder pecked at seeds. A squirrel scrambled and dug under the feeder. Everything seemed so normal. I watched the animals outside the window and waited for Joe to come home.

When he arrived, I showed Joe what I'd found. He admitted to having looked at porn a few times over the past month. We fought. Angry words flew between us.

This time it was different. He was angry too. He showed no remorse, made no apologies. This time he defended himself. He made excuses.

I couldn't understand why Joe wouldn't take responsibility for his actions as he had previously

"What is going on?" I yelled. "What else needs to go in the dumpster, Joe?"

At my words he went silent, his body deflated. He shook his head slowly.

Then confessed.

"I texted Cindy a couple of times earlier this week." He looked away. "For closure."

Fear took over and my anger flared again. I screamed at him. My words were malicious. Joe attempted to minimize the significance of both his texts and the porn.

Then he broke, and my husband changed from a raging monster into a frightened little boy with a green bowtie. Putting his head in his hands, he wept.

"My biggest fear is losing you," he managed to say.

I stepped back, confused and watched my husband cry. I couldn't understand. If he was afraid of losing me, why did he contact her? Why did he look at porn?

He stood, suddenly. "I'm going for a drive."

And with that he left, closing the door firmly behind him.

I went back to my rocker and looked out into the growing darkness. Something inside of me shifted. My anger disappeared, and the fear I'd carried for months lifted.

A surreal calm surrounded me. I had a sense of being safe, protected. I didn't understand why, but deep inside, fear was released.

In the early hours of the next morning, I woke, ready to process the previous evenings events.

Sunday, October 19, 2014

Okay, now what? I felt calm last night sitting in my rocker after Joe left, but now I'm starting to lose it. Joe contacted Cindy for closure. I thought we already dealt with the dangers of that and I didn't know Joe used pornography. I am not happy with this scary man showing up in my home again. I can't just sit back and do nothing.

God, what do I do with this? I was beginning to feel safe. How do I live with a man I can't trust? Is this the great life You have for me? Am I going to live out my days with a man who lies?

If I plan to stay married to Joe, I guess the answer is yes. I picked a good man, but I will never truly know him. My husband wants me to trust him and I can't.

The nightmare isn't locked up tight in the dumpster anymore. It's right here in today. The chance of another progression is alive and well. I went to the women's retreat to help myself, and I came back to learn that my pain isn't over. With all the work we did, I am still married to a man I don't know. Joe makes promises he can't keep.

His worst fear is that I will leave him. That fear has a stronghold on him. I thought it would give him self-control. It didn't. The fear of me leaving just makes him lie.

But do I really want to know the truth? Wouldn't it be better to put my head in the sand? No, the only way this can work is if I'm open to hearing the truth. Joe is obviously struggling. If he is afraid to talk to me, he will go back to having secrets. I have to stay strong and hear the truth about his battle.

Here is another way of looking at this. Joe gives in to temptation because he can't help it. The darkness is too powerful, and he doesn't have what he needs to fight it. He can't come to me because if he tells the truth, I might leave him.

But you won't...

I paused, puzzled over what I'd just written. "But you won't." My hands rested on the keyboard. Fear vanished again. I wondered what just happened. After a moment I continued typing, but something in my writing shifted as though I was conversing with God through my hands.

Me: *Wow, where did that come from? I WILL leave if he can't keep his act together.*

God: *Is that true, Baby Girl? Is there really a limit to your love? Could you really give up and leave this man who you love with all your heart?*

Me: *Well, yeah, of course, if he can't love me enough to stop betraying me.*

God: *He loves you more than anything. He loves you so much that he lies out of the fear of losing you. Would you really leave Joe? Is your love really conditional?*

Me: *No, I have been lying. I would never leave Joe. I thought the threat would help him, give him strength, but my love is all he needs. I wasn't giving him all my love. I allowed him to believe that my love was conditional.*

God: *Tell him that. Tell him you will never leave him, that there are no conditions to your love.*

This revelation astounded me. In my naive, Cinderella world, I'd believed in an on/off switch for temptation. I thought the power of our love could make lust disappear.

But I needed to accept the truth. Joe dealt with sexual brokenness, and it would be a lifelong battle.

In that moment, I realized Joe and I could no longer navigate this journey alone. We were fighting the chemistry of male sexuality and a society that feeds objectification of women. This battle required more strength than we could muster on our own. Moving forward wasn't a matter of trusting Joe. I had to trust God. We would only survive if we learned to put everything in God's hands.

I decided not to ask more questions about the texts and the pornography. The details didn't matter. Joe was a real man to me now, a living, breathing, sexual man. He had fallen, but I would not give up on him.

In my anger the previous night, I had left the porn site open on Joe's computer to remind him of his failing. That kind of behavior on my part hurt both of us. I went back to his computer and searched for the church support group Cathy had mentioned at the retreat. I left that site open on the screen. I wanted to help my husband, not wound him.

I shut down both computers and sat quietly. Things didn't feel quite so scary. We were going to be okay. I went back into our bedroom, climbed in beside Joe, and fell into a sound sleep.

When I awoke, it seemed I had experienced a miracle. I could hardly contain the energy of God's unconditional love. I snuggled against Joe's back and rubbed him until he turned over. He offered a guarded smile. He hadn't been up half the night processing like I had.

We lay side by side and I shared all that God had revealed. I apologized for trying to control him with the fear that I might leave. I promised I would never leave. My conversation with God gave me the courage to love Joe unconditionally. I wanted to help him get well. I wanted to turn our lives over to God and focus on being completely honest with each other in all things.

We dressed and ate breakfast together in silence, both of us lost in thought. Despite my epiphany, the nightmare had followed us into the present, and it hurt. I suggested we go for a run, hoping to rekindle the positive energy I had experienced earlier.

I put in ear buds and turned on my music. We ran out to the cornfield in comfortable silence, then came back through town to finish our two-mile loop. When my iPod played Alabama's song, "There's No Way," I stopped running, put my head in my hands, and cried. I couldn't imagine trying to make it without Joe—no way.

He wrapped his arms around me and we stood on the sidewalk in front of the Main Street gas station while the song played through.

Later in the day, I drove to the roller-skating rink in the next town hoping to burn off my restlessness. I sat at a traffic light and thought about the "nightmare" following us into the present. The light turned green, and I eased the car forward.

Wait, weren't we calling it something else?

I remembered: Our Life Lesson.

Excited, I called Joe as I pulled into the skating rink parking lot. "Joe, I just remembered the "nightmare" is gone. Remember? We renamed it."

"That's right. Now it's Our Life Lesson."

"Yep, and it doesn't seem as bad if we think of it that way. This is just another part of Our Life Lesson, and you know what? I'm full of unconditional love because today is my Miracle Day."

"I don't know about you, Babe. I just can't keep up. Have fun skating." Joe laughed, and we hung up.

I skated around and around the rink, dodging small children. I spun and twirled in time to the loud music. I hadn't felt so free for close to a year. When I reached the point of exhaustion, I unlaced my skates and drove home.

In bed that night, I laughed and giggled and talked incessantly, still full of the miracle. I believed our story culminated here. Unconditional love gave me freedom with no attachment to Joe's behavior.

I knew Joe's battle wasn't over. The fight may have just begun, but I didn't have to be afraid. Now I had to learn to love a real man.

On Monday morning, things didn't look quite as miraculous when I dressed for school. Before we finished breakfast, anxiousness resurfaced. Joe would be home alone all day with his phone. I reminded myself that I trusted God with Joe's journey, but I couldn't quiet the apprehension.

Then, another miracle.

As if he had read my thoughts, Joe handed me his phone. "Why don't we trade today?"

I looked at the phone in my hands. "You don't have to do that," I said.

"I know. I want you to feel safe."

"Okay." My spirits soared right back to the high from the previous day. "I'll take it today because yesterday was my Miracle Day."

That night, Joe went to his first 180 support group meeting. I prayed it would help.

I was excited when I heard him come in the back door after the meeting.

"Well?"

Joe walked over and wrapped his arms around me. "Well, the lead guy talked about all sorts of Bible stuff. I didn't really understand a lot of it."

My body sagged.

"But I'll go again next week," Joe promised quickly. "Maybe I'll understand more next time."

By Tuesday, my Miracle Day euphoria had worn off. I had difficulty focusing at work. At lunch I went out to my car for a quiet break. Joe drove up, hoping to surprise me and eat lunch together. I got in his car and had him drive to a nearby parking lot. When he stopped the car, I moved into his arms.

My excitement about unconditional love had faded. I'd realized that turning things over to God didn't alter the fact that I would be living with a broken husband for the rest of my life.

I sobbed in Joe's arms and couldn't quite remember why I had been so happy the day before. When I quieted, he drove me back to school. I crawled out of the car and went into the building.

Later that afternoon, I wrote.

Tuesday, October 21, 2014

I am living with a new normal, and there are parts of it that really aren't going to be that much fun. Joe held me today, just as he has all along. He listened and did what he could to comfort me, apologizing again for the pain he has brought. Nothing has changed. Joe hasn't suddenly become a deviant. He is still the same man. We have just exposed more truth. Now we are ready to build an honest, loving marriage where both of us can flourish.

On Sunday and Monday, the Holy Spirit filled me. I felt God-like in my forgiveness and unconditional love for Joe. What an amazing rush, a release from wanting to control, a release from fear, the ultimate peace in the storm.

I reached that unbelievable state because I have been completely broken. The nightmare has followed us into our new life, and now I have nothing more to fear. Joe's infidelity is no longer locked up tight in the past. It's right here in the present moment. If I continue to base my feelings on Joe's behavior, I am going to be stuck in a lifetime of pain and fear.

Why would God, who loves me so much, give me this to endure for the rest of my life? I feel lost and alone again. Joe will always be the man who has hurt me more than anyone else. How do I live with that?

The reality is I have no choice. I have to live with it. I must accept that I can never make the past go away and there will always be the possibility of relapse. I can dwell on it or put my faith in God. He will take care of me whatever happens. I will only have peace with Him.

PART III

Photos

1. Joe, a little boy with a green bowtie. (approx. 1963)

2. Desperate to rekindle that sense of Joe and I being a team, we did a 5K, a week-long bike tour across Ohio and this triathlon. The smiles as we crossed the finish line were for the camera. When the runner's high quieted, fear returned. (June 22, 2014)

3. The beach was another story. The sound, the smells and the feel of the ocean, quieted me. The childlike joy was real. If only for that moment. (September 24, 2014)

4. Writing, always writing. Here I am in the sunroom trying to quiet the crazies in my head.

Chapter 14

Triggers

Pulling into the paved lot in front of our church that morning, I felt a connection to the people walking into the building. They were becoming my people, a gathering of individuals who belonged here with me and Joe. I wanted to know them and be known by them.

An older man in a red shirt stood at the door and watched us walk up the church steps. When he held out his hand, I shook it, introduced Joe and myself, and asked for his name. I did the same with everyone who greeted me. People seemed pleased when I asked their names. When we sat, I opened a small book I'd been given at the retreat and wrote the names I had learned on my way in.

In the following weeks, I reviewed the names on our way to church and greeted people by name. People smiled brighter when I called them by name. I never realized how powerful names were. When I told one woman that I wrote her name in my book, she was flattered. Between the sermon lessons and my new acquaintances, church became the high point in my week.

Life quieted, but the quiet could be unsettling.

Sunday, November 9, 2014

I'm afraid to let the dust settle. During the lull in October, Joe started to look at porn and contacted Cindy. I don't want to live a life of stirred-up dust, but the quiet makes me nervous.

God is trying to help me. He has given me the gift of unconditional love for Joe. I need to trust God to take care of us.

Healing is going to be a process for Joe. At each step of his growing awareness about his brokenness, he has to determine where to draw the line for his thoughts and behavior. I can pray that he will draw lines where I am comfortable, but he may not. I need to detach from his journey.

***

On Tuesday evening, a bored cashier greeted us enthusiastically when we walked into a nearly empty department store. I headed directly to the activewear clothing racks. Joe thought I needed a new running jacket for the chilly weather.

I searched through the racks hoping to find something bright. I tried on a pink jacket and spun around. Joe raised an eyebrow and nodded his approval. We continued looking through the clothes to see what other colors were available.

I heard the cashier call out a greeting and turned to see an attractive woman with shiny hair stroll into the store. She headed for the jewelry counter. I glanced at Joe to see if he noticed her. He glanced toward the door, then returned his attention to the clothing rack.

My adrenaline surged and my heart raced. I slid hangers across the rack automatically, no longer seeing the jackets that passed in front of my eyes.

The woman wandered the aisles, pausing occasionally to touch a piece of clothing. I suggested we look at men's running clothes. Joe followed me to the other side of the store and picked up a ballcap. I could still see her.

Is he watching her? I bet he thinks she's pretty.

My stomach ached. My face grew warm, and I took off the pink jacket. My arms trembled. I wanted to cry. I couldn't take it anymore.

I handed Joe the jacket. "Okay, I'm done shopping. I need to go."

He looked at me. "You okay, Babe?"

"Nope." I turned and marched toward the registers.

Joe put his arm around me while we waited for the cashier to complete our transaction. I nestled into him, my body vibrating. Joe accepted our shopping bag, took my hand, and we left.

He opened my door.

I fell into the car, curled in a ball, and sobbed. "I know you were looking at that woman."

"What woman?"

The words that followed were irrational and laced with fear. Joe understood I had slipped into a place of primal pain.

He crouched beside the open door and did his best to comfort me. When I quieted, Joe climbed into the driver's seat and drove me home.

I understand now that the woman in the store triggered a post-traumatic-stress episode. The wounding I suffered from Joe's infidelity and repeated disclosures had traumatized me, setting new danger markers, or triggers, in my psyche. When faced with one of these triggers, I had no control over my body's fight or flight response. In this case, I believed the woman was a threat. The perceived danger caused an adrenaline surge. My heart raced, my body trembled, and panic took over. The trigger reignited all the emotion I experienced when I'd first looked at Joe's phone last Christmas.

Later, when we discussed the episode, Joe didn't recall the woman. His attention had been focused on me and our shopping. He had not wavered in his purity since he started going to his weekly support group, but triggers were taking over my life. They could be anything—the sound of a text coming into Joe's phone, a woman jogging past the house, a commercial featuring a sexy woman, Joe being home alone. The list went on.

My effort to avoid triggers narrowed my world. I stopped watching TV. I avoided shopping. I didn't enjoy eating out. I was in danger of becoming housebound.

In *Your Sexually Addicted Spouse,* authors Barbara Steffen and Marsha Means said that triggers and my obsession over Joe were the result of relational trauma. My behavior was an attempt to find safety and security following the betrayal of trust.

Their words validated me and explained my self-defeating behavior. I had gone back to doing frequent searches through Joe's phone and computer. I kept hoping I would find something that would make me feel safe, but my obsessive hunting brought more fear than comfort. Looking at his computer only reminded me how dangerous the internet is and how easily he could delete his history.

Steffen and Means wrote of the adverse effects of the adrenaline that poured into my system with each trigger. My fear response could become chronic PTSD if I didn't find a way to change my response to the triggers that were taking over my life.

Joe and I lay in bed that night talking about the episode in the store. He suggested I try to put it in God's hands.

I made a desperate attempt to pray. "God, please don't let me think about these things."

Joe considered my words for a moment, then said, "Try it like this, Babe. God, I trust You, and I put Joe's sobriety in Your hands. Please help me be still."

I snuggled in and closed my eyes. Yes. That's what I wanted. I wanted to put it in God's hands. I wanted to be still and know he was God.

And I was not.

After four weeks of 180 meetings at Vineyard Church, Joe was hooked. Each week, about ninety men listened to a teaching from John Doyel, an ex-pastor who had founded 180. After the lesson, they split into smaller accountability groups where the men talked about their challenges and successes from the previous week. They held each other to a high standard for purity and honesty with their wives. Joe really cared about the guys in his group and felt good about the progress he'd made.

Worried about my difficulty with triggers, Joe talked to John and learned that Vineyard had a support group for women called Hearts Restored. I didn't know it at the time, but this group was the missing piece of my healing journey. I needed a community of women to help me become whole again.

Monday, November 10, 2014

Tonight, I am going to my first women's support group meeting at Vineyard Church, where Joe goes to 180. I'm nervous but excited to finally get some help. I spoke to one of the leaders on the phone yesterday. I was so nervous to make the call that Joe dialed the number for me. She and I talked for an hour. Afterward I climbed into Joe's lap and cried.

I'm tired of doing this by myself. I am going to get help now. 180 and Hearts Restored meet on the same night, so we can ride together. I'm so glad it works that way, so I won't get lost. I get lost a lot when I drive. I wonder why that is?

Having recently become hyperaware of the way women dress, I chose my outfit for the meeting carefully. My jeans were fitted but not too tight. I put on a bright, long-sleeved top that covered my bottom. My low, flat boots were cute but definitely not sexy. I looked in the mirror, satisfied that no one at the meeting would see me as a threat. I did not want to be someone else's trigger. Could I even be a trigger at fifty-eight years old? It was all so confusing.

When I entered the Hearts Restored meeting room, a young woman greeted me warmly. I scanned the room, believing I'd find at least one trigger in the group. Someone who would remind me...

Wait. These women are not the enemy. They've been wounded just like me.

Some of the ladies sat on black folding chairs in the center of the room, while others stood in pairs talking. The lightness of the interactions around the room surprised me. I expected a negative tone, a weighted seriousness. The smiles and laughter gave me hope. I wanted to laugh again.

I went to the circle of chairs and sat.

A nicely dressed middle-aged woman called the group to order. She prayed for the Holy Spirit to be with us and asked God to guard our hearts and show us His truth. Her words comforted me.

A young pregnant woman shared her healing story. She spoke of her pain at discovering her husband's betrayal and her struggles to deal with the truth of his brokenness. Her story lightened when she talked of turning to God for strength. He had seen her through the dark time, and her marriage was improving. Good friends she had found in the group, gave her courage when she wanted to give up.

When the young woman finished her testimony, we listened to an audio teaching about detaching with love. The lesson reminded me of my attempts to accept Joe and his journey. After some discussion about the audio teaching, the leader turned to me.

"We always save some time at the end of our meeting for new ladies to share if they want to. Would you like to tell us what brought you to our group tonight?"

I get to speak? It's my turn?

Aside from my discussions with Cathy, Angie and my therapy sessions with Linda, I had kept my pain locked up tight for close to a year, with Joe as my only confidant. An opportunity to speak felt like an offer to release the pressure valve to my heart.

I looked around the room at the smiling women. Some were nodding, urging me to open up, to be one of them, to trust them with my sorrow.

I took a deep breath. "Last Christmas I found out my husband was having an affair…"

To my ears, my voice sounded distant, like in a dream. I couldn't believe I was actually doing this. I looked at the women around the circle. Their nods of encouragement transformed into nods of empathy. Eyes glistened with compassion as I told of my broken heart, the repeated disclosures, and Joe's efforts to comfort the sorrow he had caused. I reveled in their validation. Their quiet attention to my words was a soothing balm to my wounded soul, and I drank it in.

I told them about finding God through my writing and the freedom I experienced when He told me I could leave my marriage. I spoke of the high of my Miracle Day, when God told me to love Joe unconditionally. I told them Joe and I were going to make it because God found us.

I glowed like the happy ending to my story. Warmth swept through my body and my heart pounded. *I did it. I shared, and they heard me. For the moment I was elated and whole again.*

The group leader thanked me for sharing and announced that the next meeting would be in mid-December.

December? That's a month away.

"We usually meet twice a month," she said. "With Thanksgiving and Christmas, the schedule will be interrupted both months. See everyone next month."

I felt cheated, as though a cherished gift had been snatched from my hands. A whole month.

I hoped I would make it.

Chapter 15

Trusting God's Plan

Sunday, November 16, 2014

I had an awakening this morning in the shower. Right now, my marriage is better than it ever has been. Joe loves me more fully and faithfully than ever before. I keep saying, "But I thought I already had that kind of marriage."

I didn't. Now I do.

Things are better in other ways, too. I've slowed down, and I'm focused on Joe when we are together. I have stopped doing things just to keep myself busy. I know what's important, snuggling, loving, talking, and playing with my man. I also pray and talk to God a lot. God is in our marriage, and He continues to work miracles for us.

I found a song that makes me cry called "Blessings," by Laura Story. It's the first Christian song that speaks directly to my heart. The song describes my recent understanding of Our Life Lesson. We pray for good things and feel like we aren't getting them, but the blessings may come through my tears and sleepless nights. Those nights are when I've learned to listen to God.

What if the pain is really about God loving me? Maybe the pain has all been for a bigger purpose. I've seen a little bit of that at different points on our journey, especially when I came home from the retreat and found porn on Joe's computer. That was the final stroke, a lovingly painful message from God. Maybe a blessing.

God wasn't done revealing truths. We peeled back the final, agonizing layer of deceit and sin. We faced the truth. Joe loves me like no one else. He also struggles with sexual sin. Until we accept that, we are not going to have the marriage we're meant to have. There was no other way for us to get to where we are now. I'm glad we went through ... No, I can't write it. I'm not glad. The pain is too fresh. I'm still fragile. But I am grateful that our marriage is real now. We know what we've got.

I just found a paper on the counter from Joe's 180 group. The page listed some questions: What people do you have to stop interacting with? What places do you have to avoid? What activities might lead you to sexual sin?

Yay. I'm glad Joe is talking to men who are asking those questions. That's why our marriage is getting better.

My efforts to remain positive reminded me of a Mickey Mouse cartoon from my childhood. An angel sat on one of Mickey's shoulders and a devil on the other. When faced with a predicament, the angel whispered encouragement into Mickey's ear, guiding and urging him to do the right thing. At the same time, the devil threw insults at the angel and filled Mickey's head with negative thoughts.

I heard similar voices that November. God whispered, "Be still. Trust the plans I have for you." I'd pray, read the Bible, and hold tightly to my newfound faith.

But the devil prodded, "Joe says he loves you, but who knows what the future will bring. The world is full of sexy women. You're not good enough. He will fall."

And poof, my peace disappeared.

The devil was powerful. He wanted me sad, depressed, and isolated in fear. Anger and bitterness were his goals, and with a dumpster full of ammunition it was easy to turn my emotions that way. But I didn't want that. I hungered for a clean heart, one that could give and receive love without fear. I wanted to trust Joe again. I wanted to move back into a world without triggers.

When negative thoughts came to mind, I fought with prayer.

God, lead me into the light with peace and joy. I will follow You into the amazing love that is waiting for me. I know I'm Your Baby Girl. I trust You to protect me and be with me on this journey. You will take away my fear and teach me to love people with more of my heart. If I look to You, I will not only survive, I will thrive. You have shown Your love in this challenge. In my saddest moments You have shown me the way. If I am in Your light, then love is all that exists, and I will be free to scoop it up in handfuls.

***

Monday, December 1, 2014

Good morning, God. I am grateful for the insights you have given me. I see that I have been a work in progress for a long time. Without my earlier years of introspection, there is no way I would have survived this greatest challenge. Our Life Lesson has been my love lesson. I am learning about unconditional love, about honesty, and about loving other people. I am learning to focus on what really matters.

I used to isolate myself. It was easier. Other people made demands on me. They drained my energy. I protected myself and kept to myself. I avoided getting too close or caring too much. I didn't allow myself to be vulnerable. I focused on the wrong things. Checking off my to-do list and keeping my life in order were so important to me. I felt secure in my marriage and feared making commitments to other people. I didn't think I needed anyone except Joe.

But I do. I need a relationship with You, Lord, and I need it right in the middle of my marriage. Joe always hoped I might join him in his Catholic faith and, instead, I have pulled him into a different church that feeds both of us. I know he struggles with the change, but I am grateful he accepts it.

I am uncertain about Jesus in my life. I understand he died for our sins and our salvation, but I don't get excited about it like everyone else. I'm curious about the Bible, though, so at some point I'll probably get it. I have to be patient with myself. No, I think I said that wrong. I need to ask You to be patient with me. A heart can't be transformed all at once.

I want help to get through the Christmas holiday season without being pulled back into the horror of last year. The dumpster lid has been slammed closed. My husband loves me with his whole heart now. In fact, he just came into the kitchen to drag me back to bed for some early morning snuggling. I love this man so much.

God, please help me focus on the good of the season and the good in my marriage. Keep Satan off my shoulder. Help me stay out of the dumpster. The time of grieving is behind me. Thank You for leading us into the light of peace and joy. I have nothing to fear. You are with me now. You are a part of this amazing love Joe and I have for each other. You will keep me safe.

Joe and I kicked off the holiday season that Friday night with a visit to the Columbus Zoo to see millions of Christmas lights. People came from all over Ohio to stroll the twinkling paths at night.

Joe and I held hands and wandered the familiar trails, pointing out interesting light patterns and the occasional nocturnal animal. When the temperature dropped well below freezing, I became chilled, so we headed back toward the entrance for hot chocolate. Cradling warm cups in our hands, we watched an elaborate light show set to holiday music. When we left the park, I carried a glimmer of Christmas cheer with me.

The next afternoon, I wandered into the kitchen. Joe sat at the table reading. I noticed his phone on the counter. I sat on one of the stools and picked it up. Joe glanced at me and smiled, then turned back to the book in his hand.

I read through a text conversation he'd had with Kelley, his youngest. She complained about having to work all weekend. Joe's text reminded her she needed the money.

I opened another message from one of Joe's 180 buddies. Stan asked, "How was the zoo?"

Joe responded, "There were attractive women all around, but I stayed focused on Hilarie and the animals."

What? There were attractive women all around? What was he talking about? It was dark. Everyone wore winter coats. I didn't know the zoo was a dangerous place, too.

I felt a prickling of fear, and my mind turned inward. I almost followed it into a downward spiral, but then I stopped and shifted my thoughts to God and His plans for our marriage. I trusted God, and I trusted the work Joe did with his 180 guys. I reminded myself that changing lifelong behaviors takes time. I needed to detach from Joe's process. I couldn't continue to let his brokenness control my life. I'd enjoyed our evening at the zoo. I didn't have a problem while we were there and neither did Joe. I needed to get over myself and remember that this part of his journey wasn't about me.

We talked about the message on his phone. Joe hated that his conversation with Stan had triggered me. I hated being reminded of his battle with temptation. We wanted to maintain transparency with his phone but agreed that 180 conversations should be private. Joe went through his contacts and put 180 as the first name for all the guys in his group. In the future, when I saw a text from a 180 person, I would pass over that message without reading it. Joe needed freedom to be open with his guys, and I needed to protect myself from triggers. Setting a 180 phone boundary supported healing for both of us.

I have learned that each woman desires a different level of involvement with her husband's healing. Some women shy away from their husband's journey altogether, preferring to leave it all to the men. Others might want significant involvement for years. Up to this point, I'd chosen to be very involved.

Now I realized that continuous involvement with Joe's healing would only keep me stuck in mine. Finding the women's group was key to helping me let go. I had my own support and, little by little, I would step away from my need to know everything. Setting the boundary with Joe's phone was a healthy beginning to the process.

A light snow fell Monday night when we turned into the parking lot of the Vineyard Church. I had survived the month between support meetings and was eager to see what the evening would bring. The large glass doors beckoned us. "Come, be healed."

Walking into the cavernous lobby, I felt God's presence. I was hopeful. For a year, I'd done everything I could to fix Joe and our marriage. In the process, I'd slipped further from myself and had fallen deep into my own brokenness. I believed the ladies in Hearts Restored would help me find my way out.

At the meeting that night, a presenter spoke about codependency. She explained codependency as an excessive reliance on another person for approval and a sense of identity. To break the cycle of reliance on others to define us, she suggested we ask ourselves two questions: Who am I, and who does God think I am?

I had no idea how to answer either question. A year earlier, I was secure in my identity. I moved confidently through my world as a teacher, mother, and wife. I drove wherever I wanted, secure in the knowledge that I would find my way back home. I spoke openly with my daughters, sharing things that were important to me. I had an abundance of energy for work and play. I knew and loved my husband, my best friend. We were a solid team moving through life together. That sense of knowing myself and how I fit in the world disappeared last December. Now, the pieces of me were disconnected and scattered.

On the way home, I told Joe about the presentation and the speaker's final questions.

"I can't even remember who I used to be." My eyes teared up. "I hate that I cry all the time. Did I do that before?"

"No, Babe. You didn't cry before. You've been wounded. That's why you cry."

We slowed and stopped at a traffic light. "What about driving? Did I used to get lost before? I thought I had a good sense of direction, but maybe I'm wrong."

"You never got lost. It's my fault that things are difficult for you right now. I'm so sorry." His assurances brought little comfort and no clarity to my confusion over my identity.

Who does God think I am?

It often seemed that God wrote with me when I journaled. His words brought the comfort and clarity I sought. My desperate writings of pain and confusion often evolved into glimmers of wisdom that I hadn't understood until the words came through my hands. My experience on Wednesday morning at 3 a.m. was more startling than my earlier writings.

Wednesday, December 10, 2014
I took a sleeping pill hours ago, but I'm still restless. I hope writing will help. Is there something you want to tell me, God? I'm tripping over myself while I type. My fingers are confused. I keep hitting the wrong keys, inverting letters every third word. Maybe I need to slow down. There is an agitation in me that is trying to come out, but it needs to come out slowly.

Please help me figure out how to quiet myself.

Suddenly my fingers are more agile. What just happened? I wonder why they are working better. The sluggishness was weird. God, are you out there? Are you pleased with how things are going?

I see you smiling.

As had happened before, my journaling suddenly became a dialogue with God, only this time I felt the words came from Jesus.

Yes, Hilarie. You are getting it. It was time to have a conscious contact with God. Your life finally got so out of control that you turned to a power greater than yourself. You relinquished control to God. You didn't see that coming, did you?

I know you feel uncomfortable, and yet you also feel at home with your new relationship with Him. The "Baby Girl" nickname is a nice touch, isn't it? You can hear His voice better when He calls you by a different name. He has been here all along, Baby Girl. We have been here for you. Is it starting to feel like we are two people moving into a trinity? That's what this is, you know. We are one spirit, God and Me. There is a third part to us inside of you. We have been here for you, working in you and through you, God, myself, and your inner spirit. We have been watching over you, leading and guiding you. The trinity is here for you and always has been.

I'm sorry for the pain you suffered to find this out. I'm sorry for the loss of your dreams, the perfect marriage, and the perfect husband. That will pain you for some time, but there was no other way. I think you are starting to see that now. There was no other way for Us to bring you to this place, to acceptance of a power greater than yourself. You are a strong woman. You are Me, Baby Girl, your future self. You are the embodiment of God, the daughter, and the spirit. We love you so much We gave you this life. We gave you this journey. We gave you this pain to awaken you to all that is good.

You are an amazing woman who has done many good things. We have more planned for you, Baby Girl. We are not done with you yet. Be patient with us. Be patient with yourself. All is being worked out in you one day at a time. You will know what to do. You will know which path to travel. Now that you are here with Us, let Us lead you into Our good work. Let life flow through you. Heal and continue to grow in your love of God, and all will be as it should.

Love your husband. We gave him to you, to help you learn and grow. We gave you to each other, so you might build an amazing love and walk with Us in this world. We love you both and bless your marriage. Your marriage does Us honor. You love each other, as We love you. My sacrifice was no greater than your own, Baby Girl. I died for you, so you might live. You died for Joe, so he might live. Just as I did, you have risen again. You will have a new life. You will walk in this world and bring good to others. You will ... wait and see.

I blinked, sat back, and marveled at what had just happened. I took a deep breath, then continued to write.

Where in the world did that come from? My fingers were not my own. Is that why they were tripping over each other? I hear a laugh in my head. I guess that means yes. My fingers have slowed. They are mine again. Could what I just wrote be true? I don't think I'm going crazy, but it's weird to feel so connected to God. I find myself craving more.

A few minutes ago, I couldn't string three words together without backspacing. Then suddenly my fingers were flying on the keys and the words were mine, but they weren't. How often does God do the writing for me? Probably a lot of the time. I don't even know what I have written all this year. I'd bet it's over 200 pages. It's almost like I'm writing a book. A book of pain and sorrow and love and joy. A book of wonder and learning and growth. And now a book of hope and love. A journey into becoming more.

The words I wrote gave me hope. I may not have known who I was, but apparently God did, and He had a plan. I decided to trust His plan.

Chapter 16

It's a Process

We survived the first year of Our Life Lesson. Christmas came and went. Joe and I were tattered but still here. We decided to leave the memories of last New Year's back in Ohio and went to Tampa, Florida, to visit two of Joe's boys, Sean and Brendan. I was determined to focus on our visit with the boys and not to bring up Our Life Lesson while in Florida.

On New Year's Day, we woke to bright Tampa sunshine. Sean, his girlfriend Mandy, Joe, and I went for a two-mile run before breakfast. After running in the cold all winter, the warmer temperature slowed me down. Mandy didn't mind. We enjoyed a leisurely run.

When we got back to the house, I suggested Joe take Sean to breakfast so they could have more time to catch up one on one. While they were gone, I sat by the pool journaling and relaxing in the sun.

When the men returned, Joe wrapped his arms around me in a bear hug, then took me aside. He had something important to share. At breakfast, he'd noticed many of the waitresses were quite attractive.

"The temptation to stare at them was strong," Joe said, "but I stayed focused on Sean and our food."

He grinned, high on the power of having won his battle.

A bit shaken, I hugged him and said I was proud of him. I suggested he text one of his 180 guys, and he did right away. Joe's buddy praised him for his deflection of temptation.

I understood his victory, but later...

Friday, January 2, 2015
Now, in the early morning hours while everyone is sleeping, I want to pick it back up. That is probably Satan trying to turn the situation negative. I wish I didn't know Joe lusted after women in the first place. I can't change the past, but in the present moment, Joe and God are working together to beat the enemy, just like I am doing right now.

Oh, I almost forgot to include God in my battle. That might be why I'm struggling. Let me try it like this. God, should I give more thought to Joe noticing the attractive waitresses?

God's words through my hands:
No, you should not. Think about the glow in your husband's eyes when he opened the door and saw you. He has a battle to fight. He wants to fight it and feels powerful each time he wins. He feels powerful with My love for him and his love for you. You have a great man, Baby Girl. You are truly building a great love. I am here for you. When you are afraid remember, talk to Me.

You are becoming stronger. You will be amazed at the new you. Your renewed relationship with your husband isn't all I have planned for you. Your marriage is the foundation Our work will be built on. You have always gotten strength from Joe. You have an even greater source of strength and power now. You have Us behind you. We love you. We are here for you. You have much to share. Get out there and do it. We will work through you. You will know what to do, and when you doubt yourself, do it anyway.

Love people unconditionally and do not attach to the outcomes. I will hold you when you cry and give you My thoughts when you are open to them.

***

The visit with the boys finished well and we returned to Ohio, ready to start the new year. Joe's alarm rang on Saturday morning, and he jumped out of bed eager to get to the men's breakfast at our church.

I stepped into my slippers. "You excited?"

"Yeah." He grabbed a shirt from the dresser and pulled it over his head. "I like getting together with men who aren't talking about triathlons."

"Really?" I laughed. "Why's that?"

"No one's competing. They're all just good guys."

"I thought you loved competition."

"This is different. I like it better." Joe fastened his belt and went to get his coat.

The thermometer read minus 7 degrees. He kissed me goodbye and strode down the walk.

I loved Joe's new focus. He wanted to be a better man. This gave me hope and made me feel safer. His connection with these Christian men lessened my vigilance. My compulsion to check his computer and phone quieted.

Joe's purity was no longer in my hands. It never was. Making changes had to be his choice. I understood that intellectually, but could I really let go? My watchfulness obviously made no difference with his struggles and my perceptions were usually off. I couldn't predict which situations or people might tempt him to slip. Even though I knew Joe's fidelity was out of my hands, it was difficult for me to detach. Letting go was a process, and I had to be patient with incremental changes for both of us.

Our journeys were similar in that way. The temptation to engage in brokenness pulled at both of us. For him it involved lust, for me, fear. Thankfully God had our backs and He had a plan.

After church that Sunday, we put our boots on and walked to the creek behind our house. The bushes and trees were coated with a crystallized layer of ice. Our feet crunched through the icy crust into soft snow. Everything sparkled in the sunshine, including me.

I slowed my pace and looked at Joe. "How are you feeling?"

"Pretty good." He picked up a handful of snow. "Safe."

I smiled, pleased. "Do you mean safe, like that I won't leave?"

"No... I mean safe in my battle." Joe packed the snow into a snowball and threw it at a tree. "Feeling safe doesn't mean I'm not tempted, but I didn't feel good about myself when I was acting out. Why would I want to go back to doing that?"

While we walked through the snowy woods, Joe told me about a TV show he'd watched. A young boy shot and killed his stepdad, who had been molesting him for years. The police wanted the boy to talk about his past so they could lessen the charges against him. Joe had urged the boy in his mind. *Tell the truth. The truth will lift a huge weight. Just tell and you'll be free.*

"That's how I feel," Joe said. "I'm free. I'm happy. The weight I carried even before the affair was so heavy. I was afraid to tell the truth."

We reached the ice-covered creek and stood together, enjoying the frozen stillness.

"And now?"

"Now you know everything, and I'm free."

At his comment, hope fluttered in my chest. Things were shifting for both of us. I thought back to the spring, when Joe had excitedly declared, "I'm changing. I'm different. Can't you see it?"

Back then, I couldn't. Through disclosure, Joe had lifted the weight of betrayal off himself and placed it on me. He began to change, while I struggled to assimilate sexual betrayal into a past that had once been beautiful. At that time, all I could say was, "No, I already thought you were a good man."

For a year now, I had lived with the truth. I was learning to accept my husband's brokenness.

Joe took my hand, and we started back toward the house. Now I knew everything, and one day we would both be free.

Later that evening, I turned on the heat in the sunroom, wrapped myself in a blanket, and nestled into my rocker. I stared into the yard. The snow glowed in the moonlight, and the trees stood out in crisp contrast against the white background.

My mind wandered to the changes Joe had made and then onto thoughts of my own growth. Before our journey began, I may have been a bit too organized. I took the Girl Scout motto, "Be prepared," rather seriously. It may have been my years as a single mom, where a lack of preparedness could mean disaster. I learned quickly that organization made my busy life with children easier and gave us time for fun activities. I believed I had things under control with my lists, schedules, and plans.

Years later, with the kids grown and most of them gone from the house, I perfected my organizational skills. By the time I reached my mid-fifties, my house was decluttered, our menus matched the premade shopping lists, and I had established systems for many of the chores and fun activities on my lists.

Just thinking about my insistence on order, and how little that mattered once I discovered Joe's betrayal, caused my rocking chair to speed up. I stopped the chair and scanned the room. John Ortberg's book sat on the table. I picked it up. Reading Ortberg's book, *If You Want to Walk on Water You've Got to Get Out of the Boat*, helped me understand that having God in my life made things easier. I didn't have to be in control. Ortberg wrote about putting up sails rather than trying to drive the boat.

With my vigilance over Joe's journey, I was trying to drive the boat even though I had no idea where we were going. I couldn't do it anymore. I had to let go for us, for me.

I smiled at the thought of climbing into a sailboat, raising the sail, and letting God's destination unfold. I was beginning to believe that God knew where He wanted me to go. When I reached His destination, He would show me what to do next. All I had to do was put up a sail.

I placed the book back on the table. It was time to give up my insistence on having control and allow things to work out as they were meant to. I didn't have to stand behind the sail, flapping my arms to create wind. I could kick back and wait to see what happened next. I didn't have to be in such a hurry to get things right.

God had a plan, and He'd let me know if I needed to change course.

***

In mid-January, Joe wanted to visit his mom who lived in an assisted living facility in New Jersey. We decided to stay with Tiffany and her husband so I could spend time with them and the boys while Joe saw his mom. She was failing, and her awareness was unpredictable these days. He hoped to see her during a time when she was awake and alert.

We arrived at Tiffany's midday Friday and spent the afternoon visiting and playing with our grandsons. The three boys—ages five, seven, and nine years old—had their own high-energy routine for playing board games. With the game set up on the floor, they gathered around the board with varying degrees of attention. After most turns, the current player would roll around on the floor, mess with one of his brothers, or run into the kitchen for a drink. I found the game exhausting, but they loved it.

On Saturday morning, Joe got up early and drove two hours into New Jersey to see his mom. Shortly after he left, snow began to fall. I wasn't concerned. Joe had gone to college in Syracuse, New York, and loved to say, "They have two seasons in Syracuse, winter and the Fourth of July."

As the day wore on, the light snow turned into a blizzard. I couldn't imagine how he would make it back to Tiffany's house.

When my phone rang, I was relieved to hear his voice. Joe had gotten to visit with his mom for about twenty minutes before she drifted to sleep. He had been halfway back to Tiffany's when they closed the highway because of the snow. Now he was safely parked at a gas station waiting for the plows to get ahead of the snowfall. He shared several anecdotes about his blizzard adventures then said, "I'm feeling really good about myself."

"Why is that?" I assumed he meant his decision to wait out the snow. I wasn't even close.

"In the past I would have sat here and looked at inappropriate stuff on my phone." My heart quickened at Joe's words. "This time I called you."

I heard the pride in his voice. I made the appropriate supportive responses, but inside I wanted to curl up somewhere and cry. For me, this truth was another disclosure. My mind spiraled back through the years, looking for similar situations where boredom would have found Joe scrolling through his phone looking for sexual entertainment.

His admission was new information to me, although now I understand that it was part of the same brokenness. When faced with the discomfort of sadness, fear, insecurity, or boredom, Joe turned to women to fill the empty spaces. It was a coping strategy he'd learned long ago, a behavior he no longer wanted to practice. Joe needed to acknowledge his bad choices of the past in order to solidify the good choices of today.

My challenge was to detach from the negative feelings his honesty stirred up and hear the love in his shared revelations. I couldn't let his progress fuel a regression for me.

Our journey toward healing needed to be a team effort with both of us moving in the same direction. I came up with another way to view our situation.

Wednesday, January 21, 2015

Before I learned the truth, Joe was my mirror. I saw the love in his eyes as a reflection of who I was. I must be the most amazing person because this man chose me and shows me how much he loves me every day.

When my mirror shattered, my self-worth disintegrated like shards of glass. With each new disclosure, another piece of me vanished. I was lost without that mirror. Without it, I didn't know who I was.

When Joe mentions temptations or past behaviors, I am startled back into confusion. I am reminded that our perfect marriage was a mirage where Joe played the role of my big, strong, protective husband. Now I understand that deep in his heart, Joe carries a wounded little boy. He has insecurities and fears just like me. He has his own feelings about not being good enough. He didn't trust I would still love him if I really knew him. In his pain, he made bad choices. Joe is the one who messed up, not me. None of that had anything to do with me.

The mirror was a mirage. There really was nothing to be shattered. I'm still here, and I'm going to be okay. The truth is I never was a perfect wife. I don't have to be perfect. I guess that means Joe doesn't have to be perfect, either. I'm not ready to give up on him because he broke my mirror. It's just an image that got shattered.

***

I trusted God and wanted to trust Joe, but if I trusted him too easily, I would be creating another mirage. Building trust was like filling a bucket with pennies, one coin at a time. When Joe told me the truth about his past, it added a coin to my trust bucket. In situations that were potential triggers, Joe stayed close to me and checked in to see if I was okay. His awareness and consideration put another coin in the bucket. When Joe reached out to men for support, I heard the clink of yet another coin as my fear quieted. Building trust is a slow process.

Part of my distrust and fear came from my uncertainty about where Joe drew the line for his thoughts and interactions with women. He used to text female friends often. Through our discussions, he realized it wasn't appropriate for him to have outside friendships with women, and he stopped the texting.

Over that first year, Joe rearranged many of his thoughts and actions regarding women. But I was confused each time I tried to integrate new information about the past with his current, altered behavior. He was becoming the man I thought I had married, and at the same time I was learning the truth about the man he used to be. I needed to know where he stood on the issue of purity if I ever hoped to trust him.

Yearning for clarification, I came up with the idea of a written contract, a list of Joe's own personal dos and don'ts. When Joe agreed to write the document, I heard another clink in my trust bucket, and my tension eased.

Two weeks later, Joe handed me a sheet of paper. Centered at the top of the page I read, "Joe's Contract of Purity." My eyes welled. I looked from the paper to the smiling face of this man who loves me and began to cry. Joe stepped forward and crushed me against his chest. He kissed the top of my head and held me while I shook with tears of relief.

He did it. Joe wrote the contract. He understood my confusion, my need for a solid line in the sand. I stepped back. In my hands, I held the blueprint for the new man my husband intended to be. I couldn't wait to find out where we stood.

We sat at the kitchen table and read the document line by line. Joe made some additions and changes to minimize potential triggers. His priority was to make me feel safe.

The finished agreement began with the following: "I agree that I will tell Hilarie, immediately or as soon as we can be together, of any instance where I fail to love, honor, or cherish her as my wife. Hil recognizes that in my battle for purity I won't be perfect, but I will be honest and admit my failures. She agrees to hear my admissions and do her best to love me through them."

Joe's contract listed three categories of behavior: guardrails, slips, and falls. He described his descent into sexual brokenness as a slope that led to ruin. "Guardrails" were personal boundaries set five steps back from the slope. Some of his guardrails included turning the TV to a different channel during ads that featured attractive women, avoiding news articles about female entertainers, and never being alone with a woman.

The second category on the contract involved "slips," more dangerous situations that would put him directly on the slope. These included, but were not limited to, failing to rein in lustful thoughts, close personal conversations with women through technology or in person, and deleting anything from his phone or computer with the intent of hiding the content from me.

Lastly, Joe wrote about "falls." These were blatant acts of betrayal that included viewing pornography, opening secret accounts, and touching women with any degree of intimacy.

We realized that the title, "Joe's Contract of Purity," didn't accurately describe the intent of the document. I crossed out the word purity and wrote honesty, "Joe's Contract of Honesty." Honesty had to be our focus above purity. If we were aiming for 100 percent purity, it would be difficult for Joe to tell me the truth. I understood he would use every strategy available to remain pure, but he couldn't promise to be perfect. What Joe did promise was to tell me the truth.

I printed the reworded contract on colored paper, then we each signed and dated the page. I took my precious gift into our bedroom and carefully placed the single page in my top dresser drawer.

With my confusion put to rest, I breathed easier. If I woke in the middle of the night, panicked with uncertainty over the identity of the man who slept beside me, I would open my drawer and remind myself of Joe's promise to tell me of any instance where he failed to love, honor, or cherish me as his wife.

Over the next year, we used "Joe's Contract of Honesty" as a basis for discussion and clarification, and as a guideline for what we both considered to be inappropriate behavior. As I became stronger, we modified the contract to reflect a shift toward a greater dependence on Joe's 180 guys to hear about his challenges with guardrails. I trusted the work he was doing with these men and no longer needed to be so closely involved with his day-to-day challenges.

On the rare occasions when Joe did slip, we discussed the episode and what he could have done differently. When we were both satisfied with the outcome of the discussion, we noted the slip and strategies for improvement right on the document, initialing and dating the entry.

We attempted to leave no gray areas in our expectations for honesty and purity, and it worked. His honesty lessened my fear of the unknown, and my healing progressed. Having a written document also helped hold Joe accountable for his behavior and keep him on track to becoming the man he wanted to be.

As my obsession over Joe's behavior quieted, I began to see myself differently. One evening while getting ready for a shower, I noticed my reflection across the room. Unclothed, I moved closer to the full-length mirror. I stared for a moment, then put my face in my hands and sobbed with recognition.

In that moment, I saw myself as God sees me, and I was beautiful. I was desirable. I recognized myself as His work of art, His creation, perfect in His eyes.

Our culture has done such a disservice to women. Media overwhelms us with images of an unachievable ideal standard. How many of us have relinquished our sexuality because of the lies that bombard us from billboards, magazines, television, and movies? We are made to believe that our value is dependent on our outward appearance and that we don't measure up.

I was broken in that way many years ago. I couldn't live up to the unrealistic expectations I had for being a woman. I wanted to be more, and in wanting to be more, I made myself less. I hid my body behind baggy clothing. I became timid about my sexuality and stopped feeling like a woman.

But it wasn't just my body. The poison of inadequacy oozed into everything. I hid my insecurities behind alcohol in my 20s and 30s, and behind isolation in my 40s and 50s.

Now, I stood in front of the mirror and wept for all the years I lost believing I wasn't good enough.

God whispered, "Look, Baby Girl. That is you. It has always been you. You are a beautiful, desirable, sexual woman."

I wept, because I hadn't known.

Chapter 17
Joe's Timeline

By early February, Joe had been attending weekly 180 meetings for three months. Men in the program were encouraged to write out a history of their sexual brokenness.

For many of the men, their first exposure to sexual images had come at an early age. These first lessons in objectification of women for self-gratification put them on the path that led them to 180 with a desire to be better men. Part of the recovery process was to trace episodes of inappropriate sexual behavior from that first exposure to the present, creating a timeline of brokenness. When the man had his timeline written, he was to share it with a trusted person from the program. Confessing the full extent of his brokenness to another man dispelled the secrets and neutralized the shame. The man was then challenged to accept God's forgiveness and move forward in his recovery.

Taking a personal inventory was scary for Joe, but his healing depended on being honest with himself about his sexual brokenness, even beyond what he had already shared with me. He had to unmask his deepest shame and identify any instance where he had used women for his own pleasure.

He spent hours thinking, writing, and crying over things he hadn't wanted to admit to himself, much less anyone else. The week was exhausting for Joe, and I gave him the space he needed to reflect and grieve.

After a three-hour session of reflection and writing, Joe emerged from the guest room. When he came into the kitchen, I turned from the sink, drying my hands on a towel.

He carried a manila folder with a binder clip attached. His red, sunken eyes followed the folder as he tossed it on the counter.

"Thirteen pages," he said tonelessly, "done." His face was drawn, and his arms hung loosely at his sides.

"You okay?" Such a foolish question, but I had to ask it.

He gave me a weak smile and lifted his shoulders. Then shook his head and said, "No."

It pained me to see him like this. I moved closer and embraced him. Joe lay his head against mine and gave in to his sorrow. I absorbed the tremor of his silent sobs.

"I'm so ashamed," he whispered between stuttering breaths. "I'm so ashamed."

A lump in my throat made it impossible for me to respond. We stood together, while his tears soaked my shirt.

We had learned to stand together in our grief. The sorrow, the anger, the fear, all of it was an essential part of our healing. If we wanted to get well, we had to go right through the middle of it together.

I gently traced my hand across Joe's back hoping to soothe the necessary anguish and remind him that I was still there.

The next evening, Joe and I sat on the loveseat in our bedroom and prayed. The final piece of the 180 sexual-brokenness inventory calls for a disclosure session with the wife. This time, we were careful. We discussed the types of things I wanted to hear and the types of information I wanted Joe to keep between himself and his accountability partner. I was adamant, no details. He went through his timeline with a highlighter and carefully planned his sharing before we sat down together.

I listened quietly while Joe talked of the years before we were married. I heard his words with intellectualized understanding and supported the light-heartedness this final confession brought him. Later that night, the words moved from my head to my heart. I got out of bed and went to my keyboard, desperate to soothe the anger his confession had awakened.

Thursday, February 12, 2015

I hate you right now, Joe. I hate what you've done to me. I hate that I gave so much of myself to you and you only pretended to be the man I thought you were.

I said some really loving things last night. I told you that you were a good man hidden behind awful behavior. I was loving and empathic. I really felt like I understood. I hid from my own feelings by understanding yours.

Tonight, I am in pain and I hate you. I feel like you are getting away with this. I know that isn't how it works, but that is what it feels like right now. You will come out of this smelling like a rose and I'll feel like I've been beaten to a pulp. What do I get?

Here is your prize, Hil. You get what you thought you had all along. You thought you were so special. Ha, ha. You weren't. Sorry, you've been living with a cheater, but he'll stop, now.

I am angry and sad. I'm feeling mean, and I don't want to leave any of it inside of me. I hate all of this. I hate knowing the truth. I need to know the truth for Joe to heal, but now I'm broken, too. It's a good thing that I'm not talking to him right now. I wouldn't be able to stop the flow of anger.

Anger has fear at its root. What is the fear? The fear is that he will never stop. Joe has been selfish his whole life. Why would it stop now? Because I know? Because he found God? I guess these are the things I didn't say last night. I hate you, Joe Barry. I hate what I know about you. You are weak and pitiful. You, the man I gave my whole life to, you are a liar.

I know I'm making this all about me. I don't care. This is the place to do it. I'm afraid I might never feel whole again. I might never feel safe. I might never climb out of this hole. Have I been fooling myself, thinking about a greater purpose, a plan made in heaven, a love that is from a greater source? I'm so confused.

I know Satan is cheering me on. I have bitten the apple. I have gobbled it up today. I am looking at my husband's sin with my eyes wide open, and I am frightened. Satan is smiling. He knew I wasn't strong enough to stay in the light. Not with the big picture laid out before me. I'm so lonely in my pain over this.

God's words through my hands:

Walk away. Get over yourself and walk away. You are not the key player here. I AM. You have a supporting role, but this is not about you, and it is only partially about Joe. It is about my kingdom, Baby Girl. My purpose in all of this is far bigger than you can imagine, and it is not yours to question.

You did well today. Don't blow it. Love your husband. That is all I ask of you. Love your husband, and I will keep you safe. Harm does not come to those who are blameless. Walk away from the brokenness with this man I have given you. Bask in your amazing love with this man and do good work together. I love you both, more than you love each other. All is well.

This time, I didn't stay isolated in my pain. Later that day, I called Cathy, my new friend from the retreat. I shared my conflicting emotions, my gratitude that Joe was working on his sobriety, and my anger following his final disclosure. She understood and validated my feelings.

Just as I had done in my writing, Cathy turned me back to God, ending the call with a prayer. She thanked God for giving Joe the courage to face his brokenness and asked for God's protection as we navigate this difficult journey toward healing.

Her words soothed my spirit just as my writing had. When we ended the call, I smiled. *I'm not alone anymore. Cathy and I will walk through this together.*

***

Joe's new counselor, Kirk Sharrock, had experience working with men who struggle with sexual issues. After each session, Joe couldn't wait to share his most recent insight.

One evening after his session, I carried mugs of hot chocolate into the living room and sat beside Joe on the couch.

Joe set his mug on the end table. "Today we talked about guilt."

I believed a little guilt was a good thing, that the discomfort would keep Joe on his guard, keep him from slipping. Of course, that made no sense. Joe had felt guilty the whole time he was cheating and still it continued. I was eager to hear Kirk's thoughts.

"Kirk said guilt blocks healing. It keeps me stuck, reliving the negative stuff. Guilt negates the gift of Jesus's sacrifice."

I sipped my cocoa and waited for him to explain.

"When I'm stuck in guilt it's like I don't accept God's forgiveness, like I'm saying Jesus's death and resurrection weren't enough."

I shook my head. "I don't get it."

"God forgives me." Joe brought clasped hands to his mouth and tapped gently. He struggled to swallow.

Abruptly, he took my hand and looked directly into my eyes. "Kirk thinks Satan uses guilt to keep us stuck in our brokenness. I don't have to live with guilt my whole life. God forgives me."

He wiped at his eyes with the back of his free hand.

"And I need to forgive myself," he added. "I don't have to pay for the betrayal over and over. My sins are forgiven. I'm free to start again and become the man God wants me to be. God loves me that much."

I smiled and shook my head. "What have you done with my old husband?"

"I threw him in the dumpster," Joe said.

"Good."

Our laughter brought tears to my eyes. It felt good to laugh.

***

Joe and I joined a life group at Delaware Grace Church where we became part of a couples' community, having meals and biblical teaching time together. God wanted me to continue growing in my relationship with him and with other women.

I joined Bible studies at both Delaware Grace and Vineyard. I wanted to understand everything about the Bible and looked to the women in both churches for explanations. They seemed to enjoy my innocence and were patient with my never-ending questions.

One evening Marie, a new friend, turned to me and quietly said, "I feel like I have to ask you something." She leaned closer. "Have you accepted Christ?"

I shook my head, puzzled by her question. "I don't think so. What does that mean?"

She laughed. "I knew I had to ask you."

Later that night I told Joe what I had learned from Marie about accepting Christ as our savior. We decided to pray about it and, when the time was right, we would do it together.

Saturday, February 14, 2015

It's time to look at how things have changed.

Before Our Life Lesson I thought I was in control. This made me fearful about the future. I was vigilant, organized, aiming for perfection. I was prideful, isolating myself, not needing others. No community, no giving back, lonely. I was ashamed of my sexuality. Timid about being a woman. I compared myself to others, finding fault in myself, downplaying my value, stealing my joy. I was greedy with my time and money. What if there isn't enough?

Our Life Lesson has taught me that I need God. He has been waiting for me to hear Him. He has things for me to do. I am right where I am meant to be. God has a plan. I just have to put up a sail and be still, nothing to fear, peace. I am a sexual woman. People are good. People give me community, and they support my healing. I need people in my life. God loves me just the way I am. I have value. I am good enough. I'm his Baby Girl. God will provide for all my needs. Time and money are gifts to be shared. I can trust God to keep me safe.

I'm not saying I have this all figured out. I still have a long way to go. Today I learned that guilt is the devil's weapon. Guilt distracts us from the light and God's will.

What is God's will for me? This is what I've been hearing from God:

- Walk away from the darkness
- Listen to My voice
- Learn from My word
- Love your husband
- Put up a sail

I think the rest will take care of itself.

***

On February 15 at noon, Joe and I sat on the loveseat in our bedroom. We held hands and together accepted Jesus Christ as our savior.

I'd heard stories of miraculous epiphanies when people accepted Christ. They became new and alive. I waited the rest of the day to feel something—cleansed, empowered, healed, anything. I felt nothing but disappointed. I was just tired, tired of this race I had been running, tired of working so hard to learn everything I could, first about sexual brokenness and now about God. I wanted our commitment to Christ to be a finish line, the grand finale, but no angels appeared, and my heart remained burdened.

Months later, as my faith matured, I realized that October 18, my Miracle Day, had been my day of miraculous epiphany. God had already blessed me with his Holy Spirit when He gave me peace and unconditional love for my broken husband.

The finish line I yearned for was another mirage of perfection. Life doesn't work that way. It's messy. Life is a beautiful mess, and the best we can hope for is to find the peace that surpasses understanding through our faith in God's plan.

Even then, the peace will be fleeting, giving us another opportunity to grow.

Chapter 18

Hawaii

Sunday, February 16, 2015

I have a heavy sadness in my heart right now. People at church *see us as a cute couple. But what would they think if they knew? God, what if everyone knew about the betrayal and the pain in my heart? I'm living in the middle of a big lie. I am meeting people under false pretenses.*

Jimmy and Kate said they were drawn to our love for each other when we first came to church. If they knew we were hanging on to each other for dear life, would they have come near? Wouldn't they have run the other way? I feel like a fake. I'm not in church because I'm suddenly inspired by God's love. I'm in church because I'm broken. Would it be better if they knew?

Sometimes I still feel like I'm walking around in someone else's life. I'm trying to blend Joe's sickness into my life or at least into my understanding of who he is. But that's his journey. He was leading a double life. He is the one that has to find a way to accept who he has been. He has a lot of work to do to figure all that out.

God's words through my hands:

You are right, Baby Girl. It was not your journey. You weren't there. You were on the other road, the one that Joe traveled with you. You were right where you were supposed to be, loving this man like no one else. Your journey together was real. The road you and Joe walked together was done in truth. Not the truth you may be thinking of, but a truth all its own. Your love can withstand anything. It has, hasn't it?

You don't have to understand the details of the dark road. Know that Joe and I have it in hand. With his newfound acceptance of My Son, he will find peace and come to a greater understanding of himself and all the good that We have planned for him. Be peaceful. We are keeping you both safe.

***

On March 16, Joe and I went to Vineyard Church for a marriage seminar on boundaries. Three couples spoke about challenges in their relationships and steps they took to set boundaries and keep their marriages safe. Two of the couples had survived infidelity.

This was the first time Joe and I had heard from other couples who had survived. They spoke openly about their experience. Watching a man talk about his affair, with his wife sitting quietly beside him, was startling. I couldn't imagine ever reaching a point where Joe's admissions didn't bring me to tears. Yet these couples had not only survived the journey, they also were able to sit on a platform and talk to a group of people about their experience. Would Joe and I ever reach that point where our story could be used to give others hope?

One wife said, "When my husband slips, we pray about it separately, then discuss the episode together. We discuss strategies to keep a slip from happening again." Later she admitted, "The affair was minor compared to the whole story."

I understood that from my own situation. The more I learned about Joe's challenges with purity, the more I wished his affair was all we had to deal with. I was a bit shaken by their talk. With all of their guardrails, I couldn't understand why her husband still slipped and how she was so calm about it. For them, this challenge continues.

Did that mean Joe's brokenness would always be part of our marriage? It was unsettling to realize that may be the case. Somehow, these couples found a way to make it work. I had to trust that we would also.

The next evening, Joe and I walked into town to get ice cream. While we walked, he talked about perceived need. In his brokenness, he'd used validation from women to feel good about himself.

"I was immature," Joe said. "The interactions were fake, two-dimensional. What you and I have together, this is real. This is what I want. Anything else is just a perceived need."

Wednesday, March 18, 2015

God, I am haunted by the things Joe tells me. I'm glad he is figuring this out, but I hate that he thought he needed other women.

God's words through my hands:

I know, Baby Girl, but there was nothing you could have done differently. His brokenness wasn't about you. It was about things that were missing inside of him. You are the best thing that ever happened to your husband. He knew that in the beginning and then life got in the way. He lost sight of what was important. He was fragmented and even I couldn't fix him. Are you more powerful than Me?

Baby Girl, many people are broken. It isn't until they come to Me, with hearts wide open, that I can fix them. I know you struggle when your husband talks about his challenges. Just love him through it. That is what I want from you. He can't change the past, but he is doing everything he can to give you better future.

Hear the love in your husband's disclosures and use that to build your peace and joy. Goes against wisdom, doesn't it? That's how I work.

That weekend, Joe and I sat in the third row at church holding hands while listening to Pastor Frank read Philippians 4:7. "And the peace of God, which transcends all understanding, will guard your hearts and minds in Christ Jesus." I wiped tears from my eyes, tears that came from firsthand experience with a peace that didn't make sense. My life had been turned upside down, the pain of it unbearable. Yet here I sat beside the man who'd betrayed me, and I loved him.

The words I'd typed four days earlier reminded me of the Scripture. "Hear the love in your husband's disclosures and use that to build your peace and joy. Goes against wisdom, doesn't it? That's how I work."

Even though it went against wisdom, I wasn't crazy to look for peace and contentment in my marriage. My broken husband loved me like no one else, and he wanted to heal. The peace of God would guard my heart. If I turned everything over to Him, the good and the bad, I would have nothing to worry about.

The question was, "Could I do it?" Could I give up my obsessive focus on Joe's journey and just trust God? My survival depended on it.

Joe found Pastor Frank's words uplifting, as well. When we got into the car after the service, he said, "I have a new goal for myself."

I buckled my seatbelt. "What's that?"

"I want to become a rock-solid man of God."

I patted Joe's shoulder. "I'll bet that was His plan for you all along."

***

That spring, Joe and I attended a four-week class at Vineyard Church, a prerequisite for a marriage program we hoped to attend in the fall. The class taught about the six stages a couple goes through as they move from being single, with individual identities, to being married, with a shared identity in Christ. The class combined lecture, written assignments, and discussion time with your spouse.

During one of the discussion opportunities, Joe said, "I feel bad saying this, but until I found God, sometimes I was lonely even with you in my life."

I found comfort in his admission. I knew how he'd dealt with loneliness in the past. I was glad he now filled the void with God.

Later, in the same session, Joe leaned over and whispered, "Do you want to renew our wedding vows?"

I gave him a look and whispered back. "If that was a proposal, you are going to have to do better than that." We laughed about it later, but I also made it clear that I was serious.

***

In April, Joe arranged for us to visit friends in Honolulu. When we talked of the trip, my excitement flickered but then quickly fizzled out. I had always wanted to go to Hawaii, but my dream of visiting the tropical islands was now framed in fear. Images of gorgeous Hawaiian dancers and bikini-clad sunbathers overshadowed the wonders of black sand, beautiful beaches, and volcanos.

Anticipatory joy had become another trigger. When I sensed those first flutters of joyful anticipation, I quickly shut them down and shoved the positive sensations away. They frightened me. I'd felt joyful anticipation on our drive to Casey's house that past Christmas, but my elation over the holiday and a weeklong visit with my girls had collided with the ugly discovery of Joe's affair. I now associated internal feelings of excitement with heart-wrenching pain. To my wounded mind, joy was a precursor to trauma.

Identifying the problem helped. I had once heard the expression: "Fake it till you make it." I wanted to relearn joy. I decided to fake positive anticipation with the hope I might eventually remember how to feel it.

The day of our Hawaii trip arrived. We walked through the crowded airport holding hands and my stomach fluttered. Looking down at our entwined hands, I noticed the blue string bracelet on my wrist. One of the ladies from my support group had given it to me at our meeting the previous night. The bracelet was part of a Beth Moore study, a reminder to not only believe in God, but to believe God and all that He promises.

The bracelet also reminded me I wasn't alone on my healing journey. A group of women supported me and prayed for my peace on this trip. God gave me a new life, and it included some very special ladies—and a Hawaiian adventure with my husband.

When our plane touched down, my fears quieted, and our time on the island of Oahu was magical. We waded with sea turtles and snorkeled in warm, coral filled bays. Joe and I drove to the less-developed parts of the island where I climbed on volcanic rocks in the bay and let the spray wash over me. At the beach, our boogie boards were tumbled and tossed in the rough waves, and we laughed like children. I was awed by the mysteries of this island that rose from the middle of the sea.

Joe wanted to celebrate Easter by watching the sunrise from the eastern-most point of the island. We woke before dawn and drove to the foot of Makapuu Point Lighthouse Trail eager to see the lighthouse perched on the side of a 600-foot cliff overlooking the Pacific.

We pulled into the parking lot at the base of the trail, gravel crunching under our tires. Gently closing the car doors, we were immersed in black stillness.

Joe handed me a small flashlight, and we walked toward the trailhead. On the trail, our lights bounced off large boulders. Deep gullies yawned at the edges of the path. Moving higher, the wind picked up, and we could see tiny pricks of light from the nearby communities. We approached the overlook 100 feet above the lighthouse. Gusting wind whipped my hair and our jackets. The power and wildness of the wind was so loud in our ears we couldn't hear each other speak. Joe turned me toward the water, wrapped his arms around me and held onto the overlook railing. We laughed, leaned into the gale, and stared out over the black ocean.

After a while, a family joined us at the lookout and more people appeared in the darkness. Joe took my hand, and we found a quieter place to stand out of the wind while we waited for the sun to come up.

Just as day was dawning, Joe took both of my hands in his and got down on one knee. He looked into my eyes and cleared his throat. I sniffled and my eyes filled.

"I know we've had a really tough year," he said, "but now we have God in our lives." Joe reached into his pocket and took out a small box. Opening it, he said, "I want to spend the rest of my days with you. Hilarie, will you marry me again as a new man?"

I wrapped my arms around him. The darkness became light, and I sobbed.

When I got myself under control, I backed away and declared, "Yes. Yes, I would love to marry you again."

Joe couldn't wait to slip the delicate ring on my finger and explain the significance of the three diamonds. "The one in the middle is God, and we are the two smaller diamonds on either side. God will be at the center of our marriage."

The ring was a perfect symbol of our new life together.

On that first Easter morning long ago, Jesus was resurrected. He was alive again. On this Easter morning, Joe asked that our marriage be renewed. We were going to get another chance to do this right.

Tuesday, April 7, 2015

How awesome is this, God? Thank you for my amazing life. I have been so reluctant to admit that my life is better because of the nightmare, but it is. "See, I am doing a new thing. Now it springs up; do you not perceive it? I am making a way in the wilderness" (Isaiah 43:19).

I totally perceive it. I am sitting here on the lanai, looking out on the Pacific Ocean. Our friends have generously given us this time with them on a beautiful island as a point of change. Before Hawaii I was afraid; now I have faith. Before Hawaii I was pedaling as fast as I could, searching and searching for peace. Before Hawaii I hung out near the dumpster. Now, "If anything is excellent or praiseworthy—think about such things" (Philippians 4:8).

I am at a point of change. Joe and I will renew our wedding vows and formally commit our marriage to You. I won't be afraid with You at the center of our marriage. We can trust You when we cannot trust each other. You had a plan all along. You led us, so that we might hear You. You put people and situations in our path that would bring us healing and a stronger love based on truth.

We are learning to trust each other on a level we never knew existed. We cannot be afraid to be real with each other about who we are, our fears, our failings, our disappointments. We are closer because we know all and accept each other as we are. I love my husband more deeply than I did when he was pretending to be someone he wasn't. I love watching him become the man he wants to be. We are going to be better than okay, and Hawaii is beautiful.

Chapter 19

Reaching Out to Women

That spring was a time of growth for me with the ladies from Hearts Restored supporting both my personal healing and spiritual development. Listening to women who understood the trauma of infidelity validated my suffering and gave me hope. I needed that hope. I'd been living in a spinning state of highs and lows for fifteen months with my emotions in constant turmoil. Life was exhausting. I wanted to believe that one day I would feel normal.

The leaders encouraged us to invite God into our journey and make him the foundation of our healing. Many of the women in the group were learning to live again regardless of their current marital situations. Their faith empowered them to create the life of peace I hoped to find.

I shared parts of my story when the opportunity arose at the meetings, but I longed for more. I had an entire dumpster bottled up inside of me, and I wanted someone to know all I had been through. Joe understood that I needed more support than he could give. He encouraged me to reach out to some of the women in my group through email.

On Wednesday, April 15, I sent the following email:

Hi Ladies,

My husband and I are doing well, but there is a huge gap in my healing process. I've been alone in my attempts to heal, with Joe as my only support. It took almost a year for me to find our group, and I've only recently found God.

Before finding Hearts Restored, I was isolated and rarely left the house. I've never had an opportunity to share the whole sad, ugly story with anyone, and I'm afraid the details will haunt me if I don't get them out.

I need to talk about the bad parts. I want someone to know how much betrayal I've had to climb over to reach this point. I want to heal more than anything. I want to clean out my heart so I can be joyful and peaceful. I want to live again.

Would any of you be willing to sit quietly with me for a couple of hours and let me tell you things that no one else knows?

I thank God every day for all of you and look forward to your responses.

Hilarie

I cried when I pushed the send button, and over the next few days, I cried each time I received one of their loving responses. Four of the five ladies I emailed offered to listen. I chose one of them, and she will always be special to me.

Hi Hilarie,

My heart broke for you tonight. Thank you for reaching out. It is so very isolating to walk this out alone. I am glad you were able to find our group and found God in the process.

I can certainly listen. God gave me two good ears to hear. Sending you prayers.

Christy

In preparation for Christy's visit, I sat at my laptop and spilled the ugliness of Joe's betrayal onto the pages. I finally had an opportunity to tell the whole story, and I didn't want to leave anything out.

That Saturday, Joe sat in his favorite chair reading while I paced the living room. "Do you think she will be annoyed that I wrote so much?"

"No, she offered to hear your story. I think she knows it will take some time."

"I feel bad that she has to drive almost an hour to get here."

"You suggested meeting in Columbus. She offered to come here. She cares about you."

I went out to the deck and rearranged the furniture, again.

When Christy arrived, I introduced her to Joe, poured the two of us a glass of lemonade and led her out to the deck.

"Thanks for coming. I have a lot to share," I said, indicating the pages sitting on the small table beside my chair. "Should I just start?"

She put her glass down and sat back, crossing her hands over her stomach. "Go for it."

Her laidback manner put me at ease. I picked up my pages and began reading.

Christy was a compassionate listener. Her nods and murmured words affirmed my pain. Tears came to my eyes when I spoke of my fear at each new disclosure. I told of endless nights when I lay in bed and replayed thoughts of my husband with other women in agonizing clarity.

"I was so crazy," I said. "I thought if I could just picture Joe doing those horrible things, then I would understand, and everything would be okay. I was trying to make sense of things that made absolutely no sense."

I stood, walked to the far side of the deck, and stared into the woods. Turning, I said, "How could I love him so deeply and at the same time, hate him? In those early weeks and months, there were days I wished he were dead and, if not him, then me."

She nodded slowly. No words were needed. Christy knew that pain.

I moved back to my chair and she reached out, touching my arm. "You have been brave, Hilarie. You loved Joe so much that you fought through the pain and you won. I know God's proud of you."

I put my face in my hands and my body shook quietly. They were good tears, cleansing tears of gratitude for Christy's compassion and her words. I cried because I believed God was proud of me.

***

Earlier that month, with some trepidation, I'd registered for an eight-week intensive class for women who've experienced sexual betrayal. I didn't want my thoughts to return to the dumpster, but I hoped looking back would help me grieve those difficult days so I could put them to rest.

I drove to the first class on Tuesday, April 28. Some of the women in the class had recently discovered their husband's betrayal. Listening to them, I realized how far I had come. I recognized my initial fear and confusion in a woman named Tammy. She was as lost as I had been a year ago.

Monday, May 4, 2015

I grateful I am not living in fear like Tammy is. It has been 16 months since I picked up Joe's phone. There is a sad reality to this new life. We can walk away from the past, but I know the truth now. The battle will always be here. I thought attractive women were the enemy, but it is up to Joe to choose where his eyes and mind will go. He has to make that choice every day, and when he's honest with me about his struggles, I need to let the difficult truth bounce off me and land in the dumpster where it belongs. I have nothing to fear.

On Thursday after school, I drove to a local restaurant to meet Joe. He had an appointment with his counselor and wanted to get a quick meal together before heading to Columbus.

We carried our food to an outdoor table and prayed. When I picked up my fork, Joe said, "Before we eat, I have to tell you something."

My heart raced. Those words had become important to us in both positive and negative ways. They meant Joe intended to tell the truth about something, but chances were, I wasn't going to like what he had to say. This time I was prepared. I knew he had lied earlier in the week, but I didn't say anything because I believed God wanted me to be patient.

I put my fork down. "Okay, I'm ready."

Joe took a deep breath. "I lied to you on Tuesday when you asked if I had anything to tell you. I do have something to tell. I read an article that I shouldn't have. I'm sorry I read it, but I'm sorrier that I lied." Joe shook his head. "I don't want to lie to you anymore."

I grinned.

"Why are you smiling?" he said.

I stood, went around the table, and hugged him. "Because you told me the truth. I'm proud of you."

Joe sat back in surprise and I returned to my chair. "I saw the article," I said. "I knew you lied, but I'm so glad I didn't say anything. It gave you time to think about it and tell the truth. Why are you telling me now?"

"I've felt guilty for days. It's been eating me up inside. I want to talk to Kirk about it at counseling tonight, but I had to tell you first. I'm sorry."

"It's okay. You're telling me now." I picked up my fork.

"I love you so much," Joe said. "I'm glad I told you."

"Works better that way doesn't it?"

"Mmm, hmm," he agreed, his mouth already full of food.

We laughed, really laughed.

Later that night, Joe couldn't wait to tell me about his session. "Kirk thought it was great I'd admitted to you that I lied. Then he asked a hard question. Why did I lie?"

Joe walked across the room and sat on the couch beside me. "We figured out that I was trying to protect my image. 'Image management,' he calls it. I lied so you wouldn't think badly of me, which is crazy because you think better of me when I tell the truth."

I rested my head on his shoulder. "I'm glad you're finally figuring that out."

In my late-night journaling I continued to look for ways to accept my new reality.

Wednesday, May 12, 2015

There is a plan. Part of that plan is that I am married to a man who struggles with sexual brokenness. As long as I try to make that not true, I am going to be in pain. I am going to be fighting against what is. I remember reading a book called Loving What Is, *by Byron Katie. That's what I need to do. I need to 'love what is.' It's the only way to have the life I want. I have a husband who loves me. He takes responsibility for his mistakes and failings. He is establishing a relationship with God and men who support his purity. He is patient with my processing and honest about his own. He wants me to feel safe and to trust him. If I can just love what is, there will be even more to love today than there was two years ago. If I love what is, I will never run out of things to love about my life, my husband, my children, my grandchildren, and all the blessings God has given me.*

The following week, on the way to pick up my car from the repair shop, once again Joe said, "I have to tell you something."

My stomach did a flip, but I took a deep breath and reminded myself that truth was the priority.

"I slipped today," he said. "I was looking at a wallpaper app on my new phone. I clicked on the category titled 'Babes' and scrolled through the pictures for a few minutes before I realized what I was doing and backed out of it."

I didn't say anything and waited to see if there was more.

"I uninstalled the app. I won't use it again." Joe turned into the parking lot.

I opened the car door and took my keys out of my purse. "I'm glad you told the truth," I said with a forced a smile. "Thank you."

"I'm sorry. I'll be more careful," he said.

"I know."

I walked across the lot, got into my car, and started the engine. I methodically maneuvered out of the parking lot. On the main road, my breathing quickened, and my hands trembled. Anger bubbled from deep inside. I pounded my fist repeatedly on the steering wheel, berating my husband for being such an idiot. How many times would I have to hear those words, "I'm sorry. I slipped"?

"Just stop being stupid!" I screamed.

The anger was out of my control. Thankfully we drove separately, which gave me time to work through the rage his admission triggered.

When my tantrum subsided, I wondered, *Why does he keep telling me things I don't want to hear?* The answer was obvious, because he was telling me the truth. In the past, when he only told me things I wanted to hear, he was lying. The realization quieted me. This wasn't about perfect purity. As we identified in our contract, our primary focus had to be about honesty and rebuilding trust. I may not like the truth, but it was real, and it was the only way our marriage would survive.

I walked into the house and tossed my purse on the counter.

Joe came in behind me. "Are you mad at me?"

"Yeah, I hate that you looked at those pictures." I sat on a stool at the kitchen counter. "I'm mad at God, too. Just this morning I prayed, asking him to protect you, and look what happened."

I slipped out of my jacket. "But I am glad you told me," I said. "I'll get over being mad. Anger is temporary. Lies aren't. They last forever. If you lie to me, I won't trust you, and that's definitely worse. Please keep telling the truth."

"I will, Babe. I promise."

Monday, May 24, 2015

God, I was so angry last night. You knew I would be angry. You knew I would lash out at You and Joe. I don't want to accept my new reality. I don't want to work so hard to accept Joe's brokenness. The truth feels like betrayal every time, but You are shaping me with his truth.

I felt strong last night when I admitted to Joe that I was angry at him. My anger was temporary. What lasts is that he told me the truth. When the anger fades, the honesty still stands. The fact that Joe told me the truth banished the darkness for both of us. He isn't throwing fuel into the furnace of deceit and feeding my Alice in Wonderland crazies.

Is everything really as it seems? Probably, since Joe just brought his behavior into the light. He told me an ugly truth and trusted me to love him anyway. Our love is working, God. Joe is breaking Satan's rules and telling me the secrets.

You and I won this week, which means Joe won, too.

Wow. Life is good. I heard the love in my husband's disclosure just like You said. It even makes sense. I must be getting more like You.

God had answered my prayer that night. When Joe slipped with his phone, he realized he needed to be more guarded around technology. I also learned something. My peace was dependent on how I chose to respond to Joe's behavior. Driving around screaming about his mistakes wasn't going to do it. God gave me a broken man on purpose. He wanted me to stop making this all about me, to get over myself, so I could become myself.

***

The eight-week women's class at Vineyard was just what I needed. The book, handouts, and teachings brought some order to my chaos. The work helped me reflect on and grieve my losses. I felt validated when I shared, and during prayer I felt uplifted.

But it was the testimonies that touched my heart and affirmed my hope. Each week a different woman came to class to tell her healing story. The stories were as varied as the women who shared them, except for one key component. Each woman spoke of God's presence during her darkest moments. God offered comfort and a solid, unwavering foundation for healing.

Lisa told of betrayal made public and the embarrassment of having her story dragged through the newspapers. Her response to the trauma of her husband's infidelity caused people to believe she was crazy. Through God's grace, both she and her marriage survived the crisis. She and her husband now use their story to help other couples struggling with infidelity.

Dede lost herself in response to her husband's brokenness. Trying to love him, she participated in his negative behavior and betrayed herself in the process. Leaving the marriage was the only way to find herself again. Looking to God's love brought her a new life of hope and direction. Dede shares that hope with other women through leadership in our class.

Nan shared a letter written back in time to her sad, broken self. In the letter, she validates the pain and offers hope. She has journeyed through the wilderness with a God who never left her side. When she couldn't walk, God carried her. Today she is a different woman who doesn't regret the journey. She and her husband have healed their marriage and support others through couples' ministry at Vineyard.

Cassie shared her journey of pain. With a mixture of disappointment and awe, we realized some marriages don't have that hoped for, fairy-tale ending. Cassie lives with and loves a man who continues to walk in brokenness. But, as she points out, she has the courage to change the things she can. Her smile and her new short haircut are proof of that freedom. Cassie finds her strength in God and through ministry to women who suffer as she has.

The final testimony came from Jane, a powerhouse of spiritual strength. Her experience left her in shock when her husband walked out of her life, leaving behind a fractured woman who stumbled around with a heart full of rage. Five years later, with her marriage reconciled, Jane told the group that we are not defined by our husband's behavior. We are defined by God's love and His plan for our lives. Listening to her wisdom, we understood that despite all we had lost, we were perched on the edge of an opportunity, an opportunity to create a new self, better than who we'd been before.

The final class assignment, titled "Finding Purpose in Your Loss," helped me reflect on how I had grown during the eight-week class. These are some of the questions I answered in my workbook, *Journey to Healing* and Joy by Marsha Means:

1. In what ways has your husband's behavior affected your view of yourself?

In the beginning I thought Joe's infidelity happened because I wasn't good enough and it seemed that each disclosure proved it. Now, I know that isn't true. I'm still confused, but I'm beginning to see myself as strong. I've been strong enough to stand in the storm of ugly truths and still love my husband.

I guess I'm smart, too. I've heard God's voice and listened, even when it didn't make sense.

I'm a survivor. I wanted our marriage to make it, and I realized that I had to love Joe just the way he is, or we wouldn't make it.

I like to think I've gained some wisdom from all of this.

2. In what ways has his behavior affected your joy in life?

At first, my joy disappeared. I felt so lost with nothing inside of me but fear. I have joy again. My joy is fragile, but I can feel it. As I get better at trusting God, I will become more joyful. I like to think that will be the case regardless of Joe's behavior. I'm still new at this. I can't begin to imagine what my future will be like, but sometimes I am kind of excited about it. I bet I'm going to be joyful, peaceful, and full of love. That's probably been God's plan all along.

I'm learning to reach out to other women who hurt. I'd like to continue to do that and possibly support other couples with Joe.

3. How has your life changed in the last few months?

I have women in my life.

Joe and I are closer and more intimate than ever before.

I don't cover up disappointments. I talk about them.

I trust God's plan and look to Him when I'm unsure of myself.

I cry when I see God working in my life.

I am becoming more peaceful and worry less, knowing God has a plan.

4. What has been the most difficult adjustment so far?

Grieving the loss of the marriage I thought I had and the man I thought I married.

The pain of not feeling good enough.

Overcoming the feeling of being a doormat for loving him despite everything he did.

Forgiving years of lies.

Accepting that Joe will always be tempted and may slip. This will never go away.

Not being able to tell the kids but wanting them to learn about God from our experience.

5. How would you like your life to look a year from now?
A strong relationship with God.
Being able to share it with our kids.
Being open to God's plan for me.
Loving my husband openly and honestly, just the way he is.
Supporting women who are dealing with sexual betrayal.
Helping marriages heal.

I finished typing and looked back at my answer to the first question. "In the beginning I thought Joe's infidelity happened because I wasn't good enough." I'd come so far since those first frightening days. I was a different person, a better person.

I closed my computer and stared out the window at the trees, green and vibrant, alive under the bright sun. A squirrel bounded across the grass, and I was reminded of two winters ago, when I'd watched a squirrel moving through the branches. At the time, those gnarled trees appeared ugly, mirroring my devastated heart. Now, I looked out at those same trees, but I was not the same woman. Like the budding leaves, I had been made new. My long, frigid winter was over, and I would live again.

***

Throughout the spring, Joe spent a lot of time working around the house doing yardwork and projects that had been ignored for years. Awakened from the fog of brokenness, he took pride in our home. He enjoyed working in the yard and said that riding the mower gave him time to look at himself and think about the man he wanted to be.

On Friday morning, I dressed to go bike riding with a friend. When I asked Joe about his plans, he said he might work on the deck and put up the lattice. Joe built our deck ten years earlier and had never gotten around to the finish work. The lattice we'd bought was probably buried somewhere in the barn.

When I returned from my bike ride later that afternoon, his project was completed. "The deck looks amazing!" I shouted.

I walked down the steps and scanned the area. Joe often left evidence of his work lying about. There would be scraps of lumber or even tools left behind with promises to clean it up later.

The deck looked fresh and complete. There were no scraps of wood or tools in sight. Joe stood with his hands behind his back, rocking slightly, like a little boy who just handed his mom a straight-A report card.

"I cleaned up my mess too," he said.

I laughed and hugged him. "What have you done with my husband?"

"He's a new man." Joe lifted me off the ground and spun me around.

Chapter 20

Our Vow Renewal

That summer we visited my sister, Lorna, and her husband, Brian, at their farm on Prince Edward Island, Canada. After a good night's sleep, we woke to a view of sheep grazing in a pasture sprinkled with colorful lupines. Lorna and Brian were already out on their tractor in a newly planted bean field. Lorna had left us a farm-style breakfast of scrambled duck eggs, goat's milk, and toast with homemade jelly. The duck eggs were a bit more rustic than Joe could handle. He planned to buy "normal" eggs when we went into town.

Joe and I cleaned up from breakfast, then set off to explore the island. We visited several refurbished lighthouses and ate a delicious lunch at a small harbor café. My favorite part of the day came when I asked Joe to turn off the main road onto a narrow lane. The map indicated a small stretch of beach just beyond the dunes. Joe stopped the car along the edge of the sandy road, and I jumped out, eager to see the hidden beach.

I followed a short path through a break in the beach grass and stepped onto a secluded stretch of red-tinged sand. A rough surf rolled onto shore fifty feet from where I stood. To my right, the beach curved away from me, with the sand transitioning into pebbles, then larger stones and boulders, and ending with red cliffs that reached into the sea. The cliffs called to me, but first I wanted to explore the beach.

Under an overcast sky, the water was wild with wind-whipped waves. A foghorn played a deep musical rhythm that blended with the pounding of the surf. I walked to the edge of the water and stood enjoying the force of the wind, absorbing its energy. I leaned into the gale with outstretched arms. The waves crashed and the foghorn moaned.

My old yoga instructor spoke of using balance to find peace in the midst of turbulence. I wanted balance. I wanted to find peace. I moved into a yoga pose, reaching one arm toward the sea and lifting my back foot. I attempted to grasp the foot with my free hand. Steady, steady.

I stumbled.

I couldn't do it. The wind was too strong, but I wanted to be still in the wind.

I closed my eyes. The breeze felt gentle on my eyelids despite its force. Making an adjustment, I turned slightly, and leaned forward. My body relaxed, no longer fighting the wind. The pressure of it helped me balance. I lifted my foot and took hold of it, strong and steady. With my arm outstretched, I tipped forward and reached up into the pose, perfectly balanced.

Poised, amid the energy coming from the wind and waves, I found my peace. I did it. The wind threatened to topple me, but for that moment I balanced calm, sure, and peaceful.

Joe stood in the dunes smiling and snapped a picture.

A week later, we drove from Canada back to Ohio. I closed my book and reached into the back seat for a diet cola. "Are we there yet?" I joked.

"Only seventeen hours to go." Joe nodded toward my drink. "Can I get one of those?"

"I was just reading about strongholds," I said, handing him a drink. "I hate that I had things so wrong."

"I don't know what you mean by strongholds." Joe slowed for a truck moving into our lane.

"The way I understand it," I said, "a stronghold is a lie we've picked up somewhere along the way. We believe it so completely that our behavior is driven by the lie. The stronghold negatively affects portions of our lives and we aren't even aware of it. We have to see God's truth to break free from the lie and change the behavior."

"Is that like me finding ways to justify my inappropriate stuff?"

"I guess that could be it, but it also happens when we think we're doing the right thing. Like me being proud of my independence. I isolated myself because I didn't think I needed anybody. I guess I thought being independent made me better somehow. Self-reliance and my pride kept me disconnected from other people."

"And disconnected from God?" Joe suggested.

"I hadn't thought of that. I used to think church was just for people who needed it. I was just glad I wasn't one of those people. I had it all figured out. I was quiet about it, but I was arrogant in my head."

Joe sped up as the truck exited the highway. "You had a lot of it figured out, Babe."

"You know what the worst part is?" I shook my head.

"What's that?"

"I passed that attitude onto my girls." I took a tissue from the box on the floor and wiped my eyes. "They grew up watching me. I taught them that they didn't need other people or God."

"They see you doing things differently now."

I turned to stare out the window and we drove on in silence.

While driving across New Hampshire, Joe and I discussed plans for our vow renewal. We envisioned a simple event with a ceremony at our church and a small party to follow. I called Casey to share our ideas and talk about dates.

"Really, Mom?" I could hear her eyes roll. "You have to do this right. Make it a big deal. How many vow renewals are you going to have? Go all out. I'll help you with ideas. I bet Tiff will, too."

"We'll talk about it. I think I need to get home to my own bed before I can think about making our vow renewal into a big deal. We'll see."

Initially, the thought of a "big deal" exhausted me. I hardly had enough energy to get through the day most of the time. But through the summer, as Casey and Tiffany tossed out ideas, I got excited about the possibilities, and Joe loved the idea of an elaborate party. He suggested that planning a larger event would keep my thoughts out of the dumpster and focused on something positive.

We chose Labor Day Sunday for our renewal to give the kids Saturday and Monday to travel. We decided to have both the ceremony and the party at our house, which inspired all sorts of cleanup projects including staining the house, cleaning the sunroom windows and glass roof, sprucing up the decks, and replanting the gardens.

Saturday, July 25, 2015

I feel a shift. I feel safer because I am beginning to believe Joe is in a different place. Yesterday, he was on his hands and knees scrubbing mold off the deck, and said, "This is such a better use of my time from what I was doing two years ago."

He got teary twice this week talking about how much time and energy he wasted in sinful behavior, time he could have been focused on loving me. I'm glad he is allowing himself to feel those painful thoughts and that he can share them with me.

Today we are going to buy a new laptop. This one keeps freezing up. Joe is afraid of what might happen if my laptop dies. We think writing is keeping me sane.

***

In his book, *When Good Men are Tempted*, Bill Perkins talks of bad choices he made on his journey to purity. He asked his wife why she didn't get upset about his slips.

She said, "I knew you would deal with it, and I have confidence in your commitment to Christ." She ended the exchange with, "I trust you."

I wanted that kind of loving detachment. I wrote her words on an index card and taped it on the wall beside the bathroom sink. The card sat among dozens of quotes I had posted over the past year. I stepped back and scanned the cards. The words of wisdom and Scripture had been an invaluable support on my healing journey. Each morning and evening when I brushed my teeth, I read the cards to internalize their messages. Throughout the day I used them to replace negative thoughts that entered my head.

I longed to detach from Joe's journey as Bill Perkins' wife had. Someday I planned to say those same words to Joe and mean them: "I have confidence in your commitment to Christ, and I trust you."

***

We got caught up in Casey and Tiffany's party planning enthusiasm. While the house was being spruced up, plans for the party itself became more elaborate. We rented a 20- by 40-foot tent with all the accompanying tables and chairs, found a caterer to provide a delicious buffet, and sent out more than eighty invitations. We chose a Hawaiian theme, bought leis for our guests, and created seashell centerpieces for the tables.

When Tiffany suggested a photo display, she didn't realize the challenge her idea presented for me and Joe.

"All you have to do is choose some of your favorite photos from each year of your marriage," she said. "We'll string them up on clothesline so everyone can enjoy them."

The thought of looking through our photos scared both of us. I'd thrown a lot of our history into the dumpster and didn't want to trigger painful memories. But I also understood the therapeutic benefits of grieving the things we had lost. Joe and I hoped that by looking through our photos, we might pull some good memories out of the dumpster so they wouldn't be lost forever. At the same time, we would delete the photos that were permanently tainted by deception and lies.

On Friday evening, we cleaned up from supper, then set up our photo project in the living room. Joe hooked the computer to the television so we could use a wireless mouse to scroll through the photos. Viewing pictures from our dating years built our confidence. There was a picture of me doing cartwheels at a riverside park in Columbus, and another of Joe on cross-country skis that reminded us of winter adventures in the parks of central Pennsylvania, halfway between Ohio and New York.

There were many good memories in our photo files. We laughed and reminisced as we scrolled. Moving through the years, we deleted photos that caused either of us discomfort. Some unintentionally included attractive women from races, and others featured people or events that reminded us of Joe's other life.

We had a lot of pictures to review, so we did it in pieces. By our third session, we had downloaded more than a hundred pictures for printing. They covered the years 1999 through 2011. The thought of viewing the next few years made us both nervous, since Joe's deceit had escalated through 2012 and 2013.

He handed me the mouse.

I studied his face. "Are you sure?"

He nodded. "Get rid of anything that makes you uncomfortable."

I couldn't imagine what it must feel like to know he had caused so much pain.

I began scrolling. There were visits with the kids and our trip to Mackinac City at the northern tip of Michigan. We'd biked around Mackinac Island and rode a ferry under the bridge that spanned the upper and lower peninsulas. The weekend was full of good memories, our last good days.

"That was a fun trip," I said.

Joe didn't respond. His eyes were shiny. He dropped his forehead into a hand propped on the arm of the couch. His words were laced with sorrow. "I hate seeing pictures of you smiling, knowing that you loved and trusted me. I was such an idiot. I'm so sorry."

I clicked out of the folder and shut down the computer. I snuggled close. His shoulders shook, and I held him.

"It's okay, Joe." I said softly. "We're okay now."

The next morning after breakfast, Joe went into the living room and opened the photos file. He did not ask me to join him, so I put our dishes in the dishwasher and went into the bedroom.

Fifteen minutes later, he came to get me.

"You okay?" I watched him carefully.

"Yeah, let's finish up the photos."

I hesitated.

"I'm okay," he said. "I deleted some stuff but found good memories, too. I want to show you."

Joe was right. We had some fun times during 2012 and 2013. I pushed aside thoughts about what he was doing when I wasn't with him and focused on our time together. Our mission was to salvage the good. We chose just a few pictures from that time to remind us how far we had come and ended our photo viewing.

I poured iced tea into two tall glasses and brought them to the kitchen table.

"Do you want to talk about the photos you deleted?" I asked.

"I don't know." Joe took a sip of tea. "The hardest were from Ironman Arizona. I was so distracted during that time." He shook his head. "I was selfish and wasn't paying attention to you at all."

Joe put down the glass. "Be right back."

He went into the bedroom and returned carrying his Ironman Arizona medal. Joe loved showing it to people. He would place his treasure in their hands, and they'd comment on its weight or the cactus logo and ask about the race. The attention made him feel strong, athletic, unique in his accomplishment. The medal was a badge of manhood.

Joe carried his prized possession to the pantry, opened the door, and threw the medal into the trash can. The man who'd won that medal was weak and foolish, and his affair proved it. That man believed his image was more important than his marriage and the gifts he had right in front of him.

Joe's action today honored me.

I sighed deeply and whispered, "Thank you."

Later that week, we downloaded 148 pictures to a photo site and pushed print. After our vow renewal, Joe and I kept those pictures strung across the living room for months. We loved the reminders of all the happy memories from our marriage.

Monday, August 31, 2015

Good morning, God. It is 3 a.m. on this last day of August. I am sitting on my closet floor where I sobbed for three hours just a year and a half ago. You have made such a difference in my life. Through You, I have found healing. Through You, I have a marriage that brings me joy. A year ago, I lived in fear and darkness. Now I am living in the light with You.

I thought Joe was the beginning and end of my world, but I learned that You are. You God are the one I can depend on. I am awed by Your power in my life. I know now that You've been with me all these years. You carried me through every trial. When I finally admitted my powerlessness, You were there. You found me because I stopped thinking I was in control.

I am making a commitment to reach for You when Joe can't fill my needs. At first, I saw it as turning away from Joe. I feel better when I think of it as reaching past Joe for You. Then You can wrap Your loving arms around both of us and hold the parts of my heart that Joe can't reach.

We are doing the final preparations for our vow renewal, and the kids are coming home. I've been given this opportunity to be an example to them and our new friends.

God, You gave me back my husband, this man who I love so much. Help me to be a tribute to You. Help others see Your joy and peace through me. Let our new marriage be a testimony to Your glory and to the strength that people can find in You.

***

Our vow renewal weekend arrived along with my brother, five of our seven children, and their families. They were all there to help us prepare for our big day. We expected seventy guests to join us Sunday afternoon, and my girls were right. This was a big deal.

On Saturday, we set up the framework for our event. A huge tent covered an open portion of the backyard, and two canopy tarps were set along the trees. Casey and her husband chose one of the tarps for drinks. In the morning they would fill coolers with ice, soda, juice, and water. Tiffany and her husband wove clothesline back and forth under the second canopy. Tomorrow our guests would enjoy the photographs Joe and I had labored over.

Pastor Frank planned to arrive at 1:30 p.m. Sunday to perform the 2:00 ceremony. The deck Joe had spruced up would serve as our stage. I placed potted plants and artificial flowers along one side. The kids helped set chairs in rows facing the deck. A neighbor brought potted mums to line the corridor between the rows of chairs. My excitement over our big day soared.

Exhausted, I sat at one of the tables under the tent and propped my feet on a nearby chair. I watched Joe direct the kids and thought about how much I'd healed in the five months since his proposal in Hawaii. Before going to Hawaii, I was nervous. I carried so much fear but chose to fake joy. Now, I experienced true anticipatory joy. Thinking of all God had done in the past twenty months brought tears to my eyes.

Casey plopped down in a chair and looked closely at me. "Mom, what's the matter? Is there another problem with the caterer?"

I laughed. "No, I'm just happy. I'm so happy to have all of you here to make our party special."

"We're glad we're here too, Mom. I know I wouldn't have missed it. You and Joe are awesome." She jumped up. "Got to help Dan find another cooler."

I needed to check in with Joe. I found him in front of the house giving his son, Brendan, suggestions for parking. Parking so many cars would present a challenge.

I sidled up to Joe and he put his arm around me.

"Isn't this awesome?" he said. "God helped us fix our marriage and now we're having a party in His honor."

On Sunday, September 6, Joe and I placed a lei around each guest's neck when they entered the yard. We had invited everyone to dress in Hawaiian clothing, and many of them did. When most of our guests arrived, Joe and I retreated to our bedroom.

I changed into a long black dress with white hibiscus flowers splashed across the front. Standing in front of the mirror, I twisted my hair up behind my head and slipped a clip in place. I put a small hibiscus barrette over my ear and turned to Joe. He looked handsome in the black flowered shirt he'd gotten in Hawaii.

As planned, we sat on the loveseat and prayed, thanking God for this day of celebration and asking that our ceremony be a testimony to His glory.

One of the kids knocked on the door. "It's 2. Everybody's ready."

My heart skipped a beat. Holding hands, Joe and I walked through the house, opened the sliding door, and stepped onto the deck.

Music flowed from the speakers. We had chosen "Speak O Lord," by Keith and Kristyn Getty. The words asked the Lord to teach us obedience, humility, and truth so others might see Christ in our acts of love and asked the Lord to use us for His purpose so the earth may be filled with His glory. Joe and I sang along, confident in our belief that God intended to use our marriage for His glory.

I looked out at the colorful display our family and friends presented in their Hawaiian clothing. My heart swelled, and I absorbed the love that flowed up to us.

Pastor Frank knew what Joe and I had overcome to be standing together, asking God to bless our marriage. His beautiful words spoke of God's love for us and our love for each other.

When he invited us to exchange our vows, I turned to Joe and read mine, asserting that God would be the trust in our marriage. Joe's voice choked when he read, "You are God's grace in my life. I don't deserve you, but God gave you to me and despite my failings, you love me."

One at a time, we called our kids onto the stage as a way to introduce them to our friends. They each carried a sheet of paper which turned out to be the story of our two families becoming one. Their story truly blessed us.

Casey told of the day in 2001, when Tiffany, Emily, and I drove to her college. At dinner, I'd told my three girls that I wanted to marry Joe and I planned to propose to him. They lovingly gave me their support.

Brendan talked about the early struggles we endured as we tried to blend our families. He explained that the development of our "family first" motto changed everything.

Tiffany remembered traditions that developed, making us feel more like a family. Kelley talked about the efforts Joe and I made to stay connected with seven kids living in six different states. We had visited all of them in their homes that year.

Emily, my youngest, closed the wedding ceremony by singing "Amazing Grace" a capella. Her voice rang out into the bright afternoon and brought tears to my eyes.

Standing in front of people who loved us, I felt the Lord. He was there to bless this new marriage. Our marriage covenant was to Him. We would love, honor and cherish each other, as we were loved, honored and cherished by God.

Monday, September 7, 2015

Oh God, what a beautiful day. We had the most amazing party and dedication to You. I'm so glad You were there with us. Your tears of joy sprinkled down in a light rain right when Joe and I walked down the aisle as Your husband and wife. I've been lying in bed thinking of the ceremony, our vows, the kids' speeches, Emily's song of 'Amazing Grace' and Pastor Frank's words.

I loved walking out onto the deck and seeing the faces of all these people who have supported us, some of them knowing the challenges we faced and some of them just appreciating the love we have for each other. God, You were there. I know You were there. When I think back on my favorite part, I remember Joe and I sharing our vows. We shared our love of each other and our love for You.

It was Your peace washing over me that gave me the courage to stay with this man. I am full of gratitude for You coming into my heart when You did. You turned the nightmare into Our Life Lesson—Our Life Lesson of learning to trust You.

This is the testimony You have placed in our hands, and You want us to do good things with our story. God, please help us to share our love of You. No, help us to share Your love for us. Help us to take this gift of grace we've been given and use it to be a light of hope to others. I want You with me all the time, Lord. I want to feel Your presence always. I want to be the love You have for all of us.

God, thank You for all the people You sent to our home to support us this weekend. I pray they all walked away with a sense of wanting to know You better. I will do my best to be a good steward of all You have given me. Thank You for the man You have given back to me. I will cherish him always.

Our vow renewal seemed like a finale to Joe and me, but God wasn't done with us.

Chapter 21

Beginning Again

On the Friday night after our vow renewal, we drove to Vineyard Church for our first Begin Again class. The eight-week marriage program would give us an opportunity to work with couples who had experienced their own life lessons. We looked forward to learning strategies that would bring us closer to God and to each other.

When we entered the conference room, Joe and I stepped into a lively social gathering. We saw John, the leader of 180 and his wife, and I recognized two of the women from Hearts Restored. I had no difficulties in this group of couples. No triggers. Joe and I mingled and initiated conversations like we had before discovery.

The lead couple moved to the podium and introduced themselves. They gave an overview of the class format and then invited one of the teaching couples to share their story.

I was pleased to see Nan and Brian move to the front of the room. I'd heard pieces of Nan's story in my women's class and looked forward to hearing more.

Standing beside his wife, in front of two dozen people, Brian's eyes filled as he told of his betrayal.

"I deceived this beautiful woman who did nothing but love and trust me. I lied about money, and I lied about my interactions with women." He glanced toward the ceiling and his voice broke. "I shattered her world, and there was nothing I could do to take it back." He took Nan's hand. "I would have done anything to take it back."

Nan spoke of her struggles to get through each day. "I was numb, shocked. I could barely care for myself, let alone our four children. When Brian walked in the door each evening, I handed off the kids and went to my room. I spent an hour with the Lord, reading my Bible. That time was my only relief."

Brian spoke of the times he tried to stop the betrayal on his own. Each time temptation pulled him back into sin. He couldn't find freedom until three years ago, when he joined a Christian men's group and confessed his sin to the men and his wife.

"That's what it took to break free." Brian made his final point. "I had to tell the truth."

Their story evolved into a God story with a man renewed, a heart healed, and a marriage reconciled. Brian's part of the story moved me. His remorse and awakening into a world of sober maturity sounded a lot like Joe's.

Several other couples spoke that night, but Brian and Nan's story touched me. When the meeting broke up, I pulled Joe across the room to speak with them.

"You guys seem so comfortable talking about your personal stuff," I said.

Nan looked at Brian. "It wasn't always that way. I couldn't even speak to him in the beginning."

Brian put his arm around Nan. "It was rough, as you guys know."

Shaking his head, Joe said, "How did you reach this point where you can share with a whole group of people?"

"It takes time," Nan took her husband's hand and patted it.

"And you have to be open with each other about day-to-day challenges," Brian added.

That caught my attention. "I struggle with that," I said. "I hate that Joe is still tempted."

Brian gave Joe a knowing look. "Yeah," he said. "We hate it, too."

"Really?" I was surprised. "You're still tempted?"

"Yep, every day." Brian nodded. "It's not a fun battle. We all hate it."

"I thought it was just Joe."

Brian chuckled. "No way. We're all in the same boat, but God always gives us a way out. It gets easier with time, but temptations won't go away."

I didn't realize other men had the same problem. I still thought temptation was a choice. If you wanted to honor your wife, you stopped being tempted.

Brian's words helped. Up to that point, I thought Joe just wasn't getting it. As it turned out, I was the one who wasn't getting it. Temptations would always be there. I could take comfort in the fact that Joe's response to temptation had changed.

One day, I was sitting at the kitchen table reading when Joe strutted through the back door. I went over and hugged him, then backed away, eyeing him warily.

"What's going on?"

"John asked me to share my testimony at the 180 men's night at the end of the month," he said, pointing to himself with both hands.

"Oh, really? I want to go," I said, only half-kidding. I was proud of Joe. This was a big step, and I hated to miss it.

Over the next two weeks Joe spent hours writing and rewriting his story.

"I don't want to leave anything out that might help someone else," he said.

"Did John put a time limit on your sharing?" I laughed.

"Very funny. No, he did not." Joe stuck out his tongue.

"Hey, I thought you were a grownup now?"

On the night of the event, Joe bustled around the house looking for his keys, then his glasses.

"They're on your desk." I felt nervous for him. "You'll do great. Just speak slowly. I'm so proud of you. They will love your story. It will give them hope."

Tears filled his eyes and he pulled me into his arms.

"I love you so much," he whispered in my ear. "Thanks for keeping me."

A month later, Joe stood to hecklings and applause from the 180 men and proudly accepted his one-year coin, a token for a full year of sobriety. He couldn't wait to get home to share it with me.

Leaning against the kitchen counter, I held out my hand. The coin was heavy. I closed my fingers around it and thought of the challenges from the past year. A lot had changed since my Miracle Day, last October. Joe had been sober for a full year. I smiled.

The coin grew warm in my hand. I raised it to my lips, kissed it, and brought the coin to my heart. "Thank you for working so hard to earn this," I said.

"Can you believe how far we've come? In my small group tonight, we talked about taking responsibility for our challenges with temptation. We must have a battle plan. We have to meet the enemy head on."

He was on a roll. I smiled and let him have the floor.

"There are temptations out there, and I'm not gonna let them beat me. Justifications are weakness, a weapon of the enemy. If I slip, it means I have to change my battle plan. Confess, repent, and move toward what you want."

Straining toward all he could be differed from Joe's complacency of the past. Deep inside he was a good man, and he wanted to be that man every day.

How lucky I was to be part of the miracle in Joe's life. God trusted me to love and support him. The more I turned him over to God, the more I got my own life back. I didn't know what would happen next on our journey, but God had a plan.

On Friday night, I plopped down on the couch beside Joe and reached for a slice of pizza. The salty sweet of the pineapple and pepperoni mingled on my tongue, reminding me of quieter times. Before Our Life Lesson, Friday nights were pizza and movie night. The ritual had stopped when our world blew up. Now we rarely watched TV. The blatant sexuality, so rampant in entertainment, made us both uncomfortable.

How did we not see it before? Now, when Joe did watch television, he programed the "back" button to a news channel for a quick escape when assaulted by temptation in shows or commercials. Reinstituting the pizza ritual, even occasionally, felt like a return to normalcy.

Joe muted the television. "I've been thinking about something for a while now."

I put my pizza back on the plate and wiped my hands.

"No, this isn't bad." Joe shook his head. "I've been thinking that God isn't healing me so I can sit on the couch watching TV. I think he wants me to help other men."

My eyes widened, and I smiled.

"I want to ask John about becoming a small group leader at 180."

I picked up my slice of pizza. "That would be great." The thought of him being a group leader gave me comfort. I loved that he took his sobriety seriously.

We munched our pizza and watched a criminal investigation unfold. Detectives discussed the homicide they expected to solve while waiting to interview the suspect's wife. The door opened, and a woman was led into the room. She was young, attractive, and wearing a lowcut, short burgundy dress.

I looked away from the screen. "Can we watch something else?"

"Certainly, my love." Joe picked up the remote and turned off the TV. "Should we try to find something else? Something safe?"

"I keep trying to watch TV and I can't do it," I said. "I get triggered every time. If it isn't attractive women, it's sexual jokes or people cheating on each other. I hate it. I want to stop watching for temptation. It's everywhere."

Tears surfaced.

Joe pulled me close. "You don't have to watch for temptation. It's my job to protect myself. God and I have got this."

I cuddled up next to him and wondered if I'd become addicted to crying on Joe's shoulder. Maybe we both had. The emotional moments in our journey brought a lot of intimacy, but it wasn't healthy. Not anymore. I wanted our closeness to be based on the good we brought each other, not the brokenness.

I tapped on Joe's chest. "Remember when Jesus asked the invalid by the pool, 'Do you want to get well?'"

"Yeah, then He told the man to get up, and he did."

"I wonder if that man's healing only worked because he got up. He didn't lay there crying over the years he wasted being an invalid. He believed Jesus healed him, so he got up and walked. I'm still fragile. Maybe I don't I want to get well. Maybe I'm enjoying being a victim."

"You've been wounded."

I sat up. "I know, but I don't want to be that pitiful person forever. I want to get well." Something inside of me shifted, a certainty. "I am going to get well."

I thought about Joe's desire to help other men and wondered if helping other women might support my healing. I talked to the ladies at Hearts Restored and was disappointed to find out that only church members could be leaders in Vineyard ministries. The 180 group was an exception because of the substantial number of men who attended the group.

Someone suggested I start a support group at Delaware Grace, my home church. All I needed to do was take a few of the leadership training classes at Vineyard and talk to my pastor.

The thought of leading a group both scared and intrigued me.

Chapter 22

Things are Quiet

Thursday, November 19, 2015

I'm confused by my quieter feelings toward Joe. The fear is subsiding, but so is the passion. It worries me that I don't feel as needy. Maybe that's why I'm confused. I'm not as needy and I don't worry about him continuously. For two years I have been obsessed with Joe and our marriage.

I think I am beginning to equilibrate. I am moving toward balance. I am swinging through to a quieter place. I just haven't adjusted to that quieter place yet. Shoot, I've only just gotten here, and I have arrived tentatively, testing it out.

I don't need the horror of the dumpster to stay passionate toward Joe. What I do need is an understanding that there will be ebbs and flows in our passion. I need to be patient with my adjustment. I have lived through a nightmare and suffered a lot of damage. Is it any wonder that at times I might look at Joe and just question it all?

I'm okay. I'm right where God wants me to be.

The next afternoon, I walked into the house, kicked off my shoes, and called out for Joe. No response. I hung my fuzzy coat in the hall closet and carried my school bag into the bedroom.

Joe sat on the gold loveseat with a serene grin on his face.

"I've been talking with God for about twenty-five minutes," he said.

"Oh, good. How's He doing?" I tossed my bag into the closet.

"He's doing well, and I'm doing great. We talked about serving my wife."

I leaned toward Joe for a hug.

"Some of the men in my small group struggle with the Bible telling us to serve our wives. When I serve you, I get back even more than I give. Your pleasure makes me want to do more for you. For God, too. I wish I knew this stuff before. I hate that I was such an idiot."

"Joyce Meyer says we are new in Jesus Christ every day. We shouldn't beat ourselves up for things we didn't know. You're supposed to move forward with each new day. No backtracking. I just heard that on the drive home."

"Well, I'll just keep moving forward and serving you," Joe said.

"I love that plan." I kissed the top of his head.

We'd both made mistakes and hadn't been the people God intended us to be. Healing and learning from the Our Life Lesson changed us. Everything seemed new, my husband, our marriage, my friendships, even me. I'd developed a burning desire to be a blessing to other people. I wanted to bring some good to at least one person each day. That longing forced me to reach out more than I ever did in the past.

Years ago I read a book titled, *I Will Not Die an Unlived Life*, by Dawna Markova. A poem introduces the story, and it speaks of living without fear and risking our significance so that others might bloom. Some of the words from that poem have stayed with me all these years. God put a desire in my heart, a longing to risk my significance so others might bloom. I wanted to help others, but back then, I didn't where to begin.

How could I possibly help anyone from my place of isolation where I held people at arm's length? How does a person risk their significance when they feel insignificant themselves?

God called me out of seclusion and into the world so I could love others in the new way I was learning to love Joe. Each morning I prayed, "Lord, help me be a blessing to others today." He answered my prayer each time I followed His nudging to reach out.

After a busy Thanksgiving holiday, I slept in on Sunday and Joe went to church by himself.

I was unloading the dishwasher when he returned. "Hey sleepyhead," he said. "You missed a good sermon. You feeling better?"

"Definitely." I went to him for a kiss. "I needed a few extra hours." I took a jug of juice from the refrigerator and poured two glasses. "So, what did Pastor Frank have for us today?"

"He talked about walking in the light. I felt like he was talking about me." Joe draped his coat over the back of the chair and sat.

"Maybe he was. He loves your story. What did you learn?"

"Well, Scripture in the book of James tells us to confess our sins to others, so we can be healed. I hate what it did to you, but I feel lighter without the secrets. Telling you everything changed my life." Joe sipped his juice. "And when I'm tempted? I don't go there because I don't want to hurt you, and I don't ever want to feel that awful again. I prefer walking in the light."

I thought of my less-than-honest phone conversations with the girls. "Keeping secrets from the kids feels like darkness to me."

My comment didn't dampen his spirit. "We'll get to that at some point, and I'll do the telling. It's my fault, and they'll need to hear it from me." He made it sound easy, like talking about the weather.

"It will be awful, you know." I set my glass on the table and slumped in my chair.

"Oh, Babe." He reached for my hand. "It'll be okay. You'll see. God's in charge, remember? He hasn't let us down yet."

I needed to focus on the positives and trust God's plan. "You know what? I'm grateful you're focused on the new you and walking in the light. I am blessed to have a joyful husband who loves me the way you do. God is doing good things in us. If I keep loving you and God, I believe He'll set me free, too."

Thursday, December 3, 2015

When we talked last night, Joe said, "All you have to do is open your eyes and you will see the good. The bad stuff is just in your head now."

"God saw all that He had made, and it was very good. .... By the seventh day God had finished all the work He had been doing so on the seventh day He rested." (Genesis 1:31 and 2:2)

Our work is done, and it is good. It is very good. We have done an amazing thing in ourselves, in each other, and in our marriage. We are in God's grace and mercy.

We have been transformed into new creations who love God and walk with Jesus at our sides. We live each day and moment with the Holy Spirit in our hearts, guiding and teaching us. We live with the word of God giving us confirmation of our steps and redirection when we are ready to learn something new. We are a work in progress, and it is good, very good.

The filter of self-protection lifted from my heart this morning. As Joe touched me, I felt the love in his touch. No barrier of fear, no thoughts of the past. I was present, truly in the moment. Alive, unguarded, and vulnerable to being cherished. No fear, just a presence to the love Joe offered. The filter of self-protection slipped away. We have done the work and arrived at this place. It is time to rest and hear the love in my husband's devotion.

God's words through my hands:
Rest, and enjoy your seventh day. I'm not done with you yet.

***

As a small-group leader at 180, Joe learned to lead and support men struggling with sexual brokenness and addiction. He encouraged the men to develop a relationship with God and asked them to reach out to their accountability brothers every day, even if only to say, "I'm having a good day."

When a man slipped or fell, Joe lifted him up and helped him identify ways to do things differently. Most importantly, he reminded him to be honest with his wife. Secrets hinder intimacy.

In early December, Joe spoke with Pastor Frank and the elders about starting a 180 men's ministry at Delaware Grace. Their response was encouraging. All agreed to give the idea further consideration.

I enrolled in a series of ministry leadership classes at Vineyard. Using the training I received, I developed a plan for a women's support group for our church. Cathy, my retreat friend, was supportive and consented to co-lead the group with me. We were eager to get started and decided it was time to contact Pastor Frank.

Hi Pastor Frank,

I know Joe spoke with you about the 180 Men's Ministry. I would like to talk with you about starting a support group for the women. We would call our group Hope and Healing.

Can we set up a time to meet soon? I'm excited about possibly serving in this way. I have written a description of the group, confidentiality statement, and agenda, and I have a book we would like to use. I also have written a brief testimony I could share at the women's Bible studies to let them know about our group.

I look forward to hearing from you.

Hilarie Barry

Confident that I was tuned into God's plan, I couldn't wait for Pastor Frank's response. I anticipated receiving a supportive email and permission to start the group right away.

PART IV

Photos

1. On Easter morning, at the top of a Hawaiian volcanic ridge, Joe asked me to marry him again as a new man in Christ. (April 5, 2015)

2. At our vow renewal, Joe and I pledged to trust God with our marriage. We had so much fun sharing our love and our faith with family and friends. (September 6, 2015)

3. A new man needs a new career. Joe's first day of college. (August 2015)

4. Our beautiful log house was protected from the storm. (July 13, 2016)

Chapter 23

No More Secrets

On January 8, we had just finished our Friday night pizza when the phone rang. Glancing at the caller ID, I saw it was Julie, a warm, selfless woman who loved the Lord. She also was a friend and the head of women's ministries at Delaware Grace Church. At Pastor Frank's suggestion, I'd sent her my ideas for Hope and Healing and couldn't wait to hear her thoughts. She and her husband were in Florida for the winter, and I appreciated her taking the time to call.

I grabbed the phone, jumped up, and paced the living room.

After a quick greeting, Julie said, "I love that you and Joe want to start these groups." I gave Joe a thumbs-up. "I believe both 180 and a women's group will be a real asset to our church community. Pastor Frank is supportive too." She paused. "But he wants me involved in the startup. We will have to wait until I return to Ohio."

I dropped down on the couch next to Joe. "But you won't be back until spring," I whined.

"That's right. We hope to be home the first week in April."

I was so disappointed I didn't know what to say.

Julie continued, "There's something else that concerns me."

I detected a hesitancy in her voice. "Yeah?"

"Starting these ministries will be a challenge. It will open you and Joe up to attack from the enemy. Your greatest vulnerability is your kids. I know you haven't told them your story. If they find out from someone other than the two of you, I'm afraid of the impact it might have on your family and your marriage." Julie inhaled deeply. "I strongly suggest you tell the kids before we move forward with this."

I put my hand over the phone and turned to Joe. "She says we need to tell the kids."

The joy of just moments ago drained out of my body, pooling on the floor at my feet. Sorrow rushed in and swelled, filling the emptiness inside of me. I dropped onto the couch.

My biggest fears danced in my mind. Casey, her face in horrified anger. Tiffany with eyes brimming over. Brendan, turning and walking away. Kelley's stunned silence. The images continued to scroll. Conor shaking his head. Emily hating Joe forever. And Sean? Nothing.

I felt like a small broken child when I put the phone back to my ear and leaned into Joe. Like a little girl whose world has gone gray, tears ran down my cheeks as I listened.

"You may want to start by telling your life group," Julie said. "They can be your prayer warriors. They are loving people who will stand beside you in this."

When I didn't say anything, she added, "Hilarie, you can't have any secrets."

Her words rang with truth.

"I know." I managed through my tears. "Secrets are what started this whole thing."

We accepted the phone call from Julie as God's affirmation that it was time to tell the kids. Her advice to speak with our life group made sense, but that idea also brought its own questions and doubts. Would they think less of Joe for having had an affair and less of me for having stayed? Would they want us to quit the group? The complications and fear multiplied. God asked so much of us.

That Sunday, Joe's voice shook as he told our life group friends of his pornography usage and how it led him to an affair. I spoke of my loneliness and how God found me in the midst of my suffering. Together we described God's amazing path of healing.

Now they understood the significance of our marital commitment to God at our vow renewal.

"We are talking to Pastor Frank about starting support groups for others dealing with sexual brokenness," Joe said. "We couldn't do that without telling you what we've been through, and..."

Joe and I exchanged a glance.

"We have to tell our kids," he said.

The love and support we received that night was tremendous. They didn't hate us for what we had been through. They loved us. The prayers and love we received that night bolstered us for the difficult weeks ahead.

Monday, January 11, 2016

It is 2 a.m. and I am not happy to be awake this early. I took a sleeping pill because I was afraid my mind would wander after sharing with our life group last night.

I just heard a snowplow go by. They are loud. I guess that's what woke me.

Are we doing the right thing? Lord, Are we selfish to bring the kids into this? Would it really be better to keep them in the dark? If we can't do ministry without telling them, are we selfish to insist on doing ministry? Would we be better parents if we kept the secret to ourselves? Are we meant to put this burden on those we love?

Satan is putting doubt in my heart. He is after me, telling me it's wrong to share our pain. It is wrong to tear down the image Joe's kids have of their father as invincible. Wrong to crush the fairy tale dream of the perfect marriage.

Girls, I'm sorry, but you will never be Cinderella. There is no ball, no Prince Charming. He is a liar and a cheater. My Prince Charming fooled all of us. He wasn't the knight in shining armor he pretended to be.

God's words through my hands:

No, Baby Girl, he was human, and you couldn't fix him. Only the Holy Spirit could bring him into the light. Only I could rescue him. There is falseness in every relationship. You all fall short. There are no perfect people.

I am the foundation on which Joe will build his manhood. He had to learn that. You all must learn that. None of you can find balance without Me. Your kids need to learn, too. Your story will help them. You believe it's impossible but look at your journey. I can work miracles in your children's lives, as well.

But it is never easy. My children are stubborn. They rarely come to me without pain. I must be birthed into people's lives. They must be desperate. Yours is a story of My glory. Your husband was broken, and I am healing his heart. Do your children deserve less?

Allow the boys to really see their father, his self-doubt and fear. Let them see that a broken man can change, can move into the light. Trust Me.

Your girls have been watching you, wondering what happened. They love you and they love Joe. You do them no service in hiding My glory from them. One day, they will need your example of faith for their own trials.

The pain of the truth will fade. The lessons will live in their hearts. They will know you needed Me to save your marriage. I can save them, too, if they only ask. It won't be easy, Baby Girl, but trust them. Trust their love for you. This is right, Baby Girl. Have no fears. This is right.

***

With the blessings of our prayer warriors in place, we were ready to create a plan. On Wednesday, January 13, Joe and I mapped out a timeline for sharing our story. We decided to share with the kids, my three siblings, and all of their spouses. We wanted to ensure that everyone heard our disclosure within the shortest time frame possible.

Our goal was two weeks. We would ask them to keep our story to themselves for that time period.

Our seven kids lived in Ohio, West Virginia, New York, New Jersey, Florida, and Alaska. My siblings were in California, Canada, and the state of Washington. Speaking to all of them within two weeks would be challenging, but we wanted them to be able to process with each other—and we wanted to get it over with.

Tiffany invited us to New York for Valentine's weekend, so we used that as our pivotal weekend. We would speak to Emily and Kelley face-to-face in Ohio on Saturday, February 6. The following weekend we would drive to New York to speak with Casey and Tiffany, also in person. Between those two weekends and the next week we would schedule phone and Skype sessions with everyone else.

Despite the encouragement we received from our life group, we were petrified. I dreaded telling the kids we had deceived them for two years. Would the girls hate me when they learned I had been lying? Would they fear for their own marriages?

Our story, like a powerful earthquake, had the potential to undermine the foundation of trust in our family. Joe feared this could end his relationship with my girls and negatively impact his relationships with his own kids.

I thought of Christmas next year. What if some of them refused to ever come to our house again? We might never have another family Christmas.

Joe and I held each other close and prayed for the strength to trust God's plan.

We spent the next week writing and rewriting our story. Our goal was to share general information about Joe's betrayal, but more importantly, to help them see how God's love healed us. The predominant message we hoped to give them was a story for God's glory.

My sister, Lorna, and her husband were first on the list. We thought they would be the most forgiving toward Joe. The conversation with them would be our practice session for telling everyone else.

On Monday, January 18, Joe and I sat at the kitchen table, staring at my phone. My foot tapped nervously. "You ready?"

Joe nodded.

I dialed Lorna's number and put the call on speaker.

The phone rang three, then four times.

"Maybe they aren't home," I said.

"Hello?" Lorna's voice sang out.

We both let out the breath. Here we go.

After a rushed greeting with Lorna, I said, "We need to talk to you and Brian about some issues in our marriage. We're fine but want to share. Can Brian come to the phone?"

"You bet." We heard Lorna rush away from the phone and then shout into the yard for her husband.

While we waited our eyes met. "We're gonna be okay," I said, taking Joe's hand.

He gave me a single nod.

Lorna picked up. "Okay, we're here. Shoot."

Joe cleared his throat. "I'm going to read this, okay?"

"Of course."

In a shaky voice, he began. "Through a large part of my life, I've had an issue, some might call it an addiction to pornography. With the internet, porn became more available. I've struggled with this for a long time. Hil knew nothing about it because I kept it secret, and I learned to lie really well…"

Joe continued the story of his progression into an affair. Hearing only silence from the other end, we checked with Lorna and Brian a few times to make sure we hadn't lost connection. They assured us they were still there and listening to every word.

When Joe finished talking, I shared about my pain and loneliness, but quickly shifted into the message I wanted to convey. "We began going to church, and then I had my Miracle Day…"

Lorna and Brian heard us, affirmed our journey with God, and focused on Joe having turned his life around.

"Everyone makes mistakes," Lorna said.

We ended the call promising to talk soon.

Joe and I stood and wrapped our arms around each other. I snuggled in and relief swept through my body like a swoosh of fresh air.

"We did it," Joe said, quietly. "And they don't hate me."

Joe decided to go outside and ride around on the mower to burn off his nervous energy. There were plenty of leaves waiting to be chopped up and dispersed. We kissed and he left the room.

I sat back and stared at the phone. The elation of moments earlier evaporated. My sister's closing remark echoed in my mind. "Everyone makes mistakes."

Wait a minute. That's it? That's all I get? Lorna pats Joe on the head and I get nothing. This wasn't just a mistake. My life has been a horrible, frightening nightmare, and I need my sister to know that.

I picked up the phone and called her back. Lorna answered on the first ring.

"We didn't share all of it," I said. "I need you to hear the whole story. I want you know what I've been through. It was a nightmare." My voice choked, and I began to cry. "I couldn't understand what happened to my beautiful life. Joe became a stranger, and yet he was the only one I could turn to. I was scared all the time. It's like the world went dark and I didn't know what to do."

Over the next three hours, I emptied the dumpster as I had for Christy ten months earlier, out on the back deck. As my story unfolded, Lorna acknowledged that the betrayal was much bigger than she imagined.

"I can't believe you've been carrying all of this on your own." She paused. "You poor thing." I heard the sorrow in her voice. She meant it. Now, she understood what I had suffered, and I was glad for that.

"I'm surprised you stayed." Lorna paused again. "Why didn't you leave?"

I looked out through the sliding door into the yard. At that moment, Joe rode past on the mower. He noticed me and held up his left hand, signing, "I love you."

I smiled. "I couldn't believe Joe wasn't the man I thought he was, and I didn't want to lose my best friend. When God told me to love him unconditionally, it was what I wanted to hear. I wanted someone to tell me to stay."

"Okay. I can support that. I'm glad you were strong enough to stay."

"Thanks for hearing me, and for letting me spill out my stupid dumpster. I needed my sis to understand."

"I'll be happy to listen any time. You didn't deserve any of it. And I think you are amazing for being able to save your marriage."

That week Joe and I shared our story with a few select friends, and by the following week I felt different. The weight of secrecy had lightened. God told us it was time to spill out the dumpster for His glory, and each time we did, another piece of my fragmented world shifted into a familiar place.

Thursday, January 28, 2016

I just read, "In Him we were also chosen, having been predestined according to the plan of Him who works out everything in conformity with the purpose of His will" (Ephesians 1:11-12).

My attention has been focused on the miracle in Joe's life and the miracle of our marriage being restored. I believed my purpose has been in helping Joe heal. Maybe I should focus on my own journey, free and clear of Joe. What if I concentrate on the changes and miracles God has in mind for my life?

The Scripture says we were chosen. I was chosen and predestined to be part of God's plan for His purpose. Maybe saving Joe has not been the whole purpose of my life.

It's like I'm waiting for someone to say, "Hilarie, you are important. You have value all by yourself. This trauma was for your growth." Could God really have planned my life just for Joe's healing? No, of course not.

God's words through my hands:

Baby Girl, you matter. You matter as much as Joe. The journey was for both of you. If you admit to growing and finding a purpose for your life, it does not make even one small act of the betrayal acceptable.

This was for you free and clear of your husband. We wanted you to know Us.

You were chosen. We have more for you to do. We broke you so you would be Ours. We wanted you to be a testament to Our glory.

You will have the peace, joy, and love you desire. Then see where We will lead. The journey will amaze you. Trust Us. We have always been with you. Do not be afraid.

"Now then, stand still and watch this great thing that the Lord is about to do before your eyes" (1 Samuel 12:16).

Chapter 24

Telling the Kids

The two-week timeframe for sharing with the kids began Saturday afternoon, February 6. Kelley came up from West Virginia for the weekend. Emily lived close by and stopped in to visit with her. The girls chatted at the kitchen table, eating macaroni and cheese. I busied myself at the sink. Anxious jitters fluttered in my stomach.

Joe interrupted the girls' conversation and asked if we could speak with them when they finished lunch. Kelley gave her stepsister a questioning glance. Emily shrugged and quickly emptied her bowl.

Joe went to his desk to collect the pages we had labored over, then sat beside me in his usual place at the head of the table. He reached under the table, took my hand, and held it.

The girls rushed their dishes into the dishwasher. Emily chose to sit in the chair next to mine, and Kelly sat across from Joe.

The room hummed with unvoiced tension. I had difficulty breathing the heavy air. I looked at the girls. Kelley's brows were drawn together in a line of concern. I feared Joe's words would shatter the hero worship she had for her father. Emily waited patiently, appearing oblivious to the strain the rest of us felt.

"First off," I managed, "Joe and I are fine, but for a while we weren't, and we want to tell you what happened." My voice wavered as I rushed through our preamble. "This isn't new. It all started more than two years ago."

I nodded toward Joe.

He picked up the stapled pages and read. "We've made reference to…" He cleared his throat and glanced up at Kelley. The papers in his hands shook. He put them on the table. "We've made reference to significant challenges in our marriage…"

The trembling in my stomach moved into my chest and down my arms. A weight settled in my throat, making it difficult to swallow.

He continued, "Through a large part of my life I've had an issue, some might call it an addiction to pornography."

I listened to Joe through the buzzing in my ears, white noise created by the adrenalin that flowed freely through my veins.

"Just over two years ago your mom, Hil, discovered I was having an affair..."

I watched their reactions. Emily leaned in, placing her arms on the table, her eyes hardened, her lips slack. Kelley sat back in her chair. She nodded almost imperceptibly.

When Joe finished the first part of our story, Emily glared, silently. I hoped my piece of the story would help her understand that God had fixed everything.

"I am so sorry for the pain our story may cause you," I read. "We had to tell you because it has been a dark cloud blocking the truth in our relationships with you. Our marriage is stronger than it has ever been, but our marriage is obviously far from perfect, and we couldn't let that perfection lie continue. The last two years have been the most difficult of my life..."

I spoke of my shock and anger, and how my world came crashing down. I explained that I didn't want to leave Joe, despite the pain.

"We were both so desperate to make it work, that we started listening to God. God told me what to do through my writing. He told me to walk away from the past and love Joe unconditionally."

I looked from Emily to Kelley, hoping they understood. "It's easy to love someone when everything is going well. We learned to love each other in the middle of a nightmare. We hope with time you will see this for the love story that it is."

I handed the papers back to Joe.

He straightened their edges and said, "One day, about six months after this all came to light, we saw a sign in an antique shop. The sign read, 'A perfect marriage is just two imperfect people who refuse to give up on each other.' We believed those words were there for us because that's what we did. We refused to give up."

Joe took off his glasses and lay them on top of the papers. He looked directly at Emily. "I'm sorry for what I did to your mom."

I sat back, dropping my hands into my lap. *We did it. It's over. We told them.* For a few short moments I rode on a high of relief.

Emily shifted in her chair and turned to me. "I'm angry at Joe for what he did to you."

I leaned over and rubbed her arm. "I know, Em."

Kelley said, "I'm not mad at you, Dad. I knew."

We all turned to Kelley.

"A few weeks ago, I borrowed Hil's laptop. I saw 'sex addiction' in the search history. I thought you guys were going to tell us you were getting divorced."

My mouth dropped. She knew?

Kelley rose from the table. "I'm glad I was wrong."

The words felt like a careless afterthought.

I feared the truth might damage the bond she and Joe shared, but her nonchalance confused me. I lost my focus on our God story. *What about the betrayal? What about me?*

I couldn't help asking, "With everything you've heard, do you feel a little sorry for me?"

"Well," she pushed in her chair, "from what I can see it all worked out okay."

Kelley went to the refrigerator and got herself a drink, ending the conversation.

I sat there, at a loss for words.

Emily motioned for me to follow her, and we left the room to talk privately.

Sunday, February 7, 2016

Now I'm questioning the wisdom of our disclosure. After today, Joe and I are pulling away from each other. I was afraid of this from the beginning. I didn't want to rip apart our family, and I feel a tear beginning right at the bottom with the two youngest girls. I am projecting that Kelley wishes we had broken up. Joe is projecting that Emily wishes the same thing. I want to defend Emily, and I'm sure he wants to defend Kelley.

God, don't let this tear us apart.

Joe told me the little boy in him wanted to lash out when Emily said she was angry, but he knew he had to accept her anger.

Are we doing the right thing? Are we strong enough for this?

I'm scared again, but too many things have pointed us toward sharing with the kids. This isn't about us. This is for Your glory. You want the dumpster spilled out on the ground. You do not want us to hide.

The sharing will be painful. It is already painful in ways I hadn't imagined. Kelley loves me, but she cannot give me what I need right now. Emily can. She can stand by me and comfort me.

You are turning this into another love lesson. It is so hard to let You have Your way with my life, but for now I feel peaceful. Thank you.

Two days later doubt continued to plague my thoughts.

Tuesday, February 9, 2016

Oh, God, I see Satan's at work in my heart this morning, and we haven't even talked to the older girls yet. When I imagine the looks on their faces, I turn it into disappointment in me, disappointment in the choice I have made to stay with this man. I feel their displeasure seeping into my own perceptions of Joe and our marriage. My 'God story' gets reduced to a dirty disappointment.

We believed everyone would hear our story and think, "Wow. God really wanted them to make it." Casey and Tiffany are not going to think that. They won't see the miracle at all. They won't understand that You told me to love Joe unconditionally. They won't notice that by Your grace Joe has turned his life around.

They will only see what is in their own hearts, the sorrow and the disenchantment. They thought I was safe with Joe. He was everything they would want for me. The girls were so proud of our marriage and wanted that for themselves. They will be so disappointed.

Oh, Lord, protect me from taking their feelings into my heart. Help me stand in the storm of their pain. Help me stand strong beside Joe, finding a balance between supporting their hearts and protecting him. Protect my heart, and don't let their pain put a wedge between Joe and me. I am so scared, God. Help me to trust You.

Do we really have to do this? Can we just change our minds? I'm afraid. Please help me.

On Saturday morning at 4 a.m., Joe and I climbed into the Malibu with a plan to arrive at Tiffany's house around noon. Casey would join us there at 2. We told them we wanted to discuss something and asked that their husbands join us.

My stomach ached the entire car ride. Sharing with Casey and Tiffany would be the most difficult session we faced. They were extremely protective of me and they loved Joe. As the patriarch of our family, he set the example for how they wanted to be treated. Both girls saw our "perfect" marriage as an ideal to strive for.

Joe and I feared we were heading into the ultimate skirmish. Casey, a lawyer by trade, didn't hold back when a situation warranted confrontation. With Tiffany backing her up, it could get ugly.

At 2:15, the four of us, Casey, Tiffany, Joe, and I, carried drinks to the dining room table. Their husbands had been called to other issues. I wondered if we should wait or change the plan but realized God must want us to speak with the girls alone. Tiffany and Casey laughed as they shared antics from their most recent girls' night out. Joe and I did our best to show interest in their stories.

Casey took off her sweatshirt and draped it over the back of her chair. Directing her attention to Joe and me, she said, "So, what's going on with you guys?"

I took a sip of my diet cola. The drink burned going down. Bitterness rose in the back of my throat. I thought I might get sick.

I swallowed and robotically spoke the words I used to start our talk with Emily and Kelley. "Joe and I are fine, but for a while we weren't, and we want to tell you what happened. This all started more than two years ago, and we're fine now."

The laughter of moments earlier died. The girls looked from me to Joe, concern written on their faces.

Joe took the papers from his lap and placed them on the table in front of him.

My stomach dropped. A chill ran through my body like ice water being poured down my back.

Confusion crept across Casey and Tiffany's faces.

Joe adjusted the papers and began. His voice trembled. He spoke of his efforts to hide his pornography usage and its slow progression over the years of our marriage. Joe blinked, trying to hold back tears. "Just over two years ago, your mom discovered I was having an affair."

Casey stared at Joe, her jaw slack in open-mouthed shock. The sparkle in Tiffany's eyes dulled and tears welled.

My mind spun away from the room. I was there, but I wasn't. *I can't believe this is happening. It's like watching a bad movie. Joe and Tiffany are crying. I don't want to be here. I hate this. What we are doing to our family? I don't want to do this to my girls.*

"While I was in it," Joe continued, "I knew the affair could cost me my marriage, but I lived in a fog of denial. When your mom found out and I saw the pain on her face, it was like getting slammed in the forehead with a 2x4. The fog lifted, and I realized how much I hurt the one person who is most important to me in all the world. In that moment, I knew I would do whatever it took to keep her and our marriage."

He spoke of his self-examination and his efforts to be honest with himself and with me. He spoke of how badly he wanted to take away my pain.

I watched helplessly as Joe confessed his betrayal to my daughters. Now Casey and Tiffany understood they had been deceived. Joe wasn't the great husband and stepfather they believed him to be. He had lied to all of us.

Casey found her voice, her face a mask of sorrow. "Oh, Mom."

Joe slid the pages in front of me.

This was my opportunity to make things better. *Please, Lord, please let them see how You saved me. Help them understand that we're okay because of You.*

I wiped my eyes with a tissue and put on my glasses. I read slowly, attempting to soothe the girls with my voice.

"Like you, I was shocked. I was furious, scared, numb. I was sick. My world came crashing down and everything I believed about my life disappeared. I thought our marriage was perfect." I shook my head. "It wasn't. Joe was broken." My voice faltered. "I was so confused. I thought I should leave, but I didn't want to. Neither of us wanted to end our marriage, so we fought for it. I fought to love Joe despite my pain, and he fought to comfort me and to change. For close to a year we tried to figure this out by ourselves, but we continued to struggle."

The words on the paper blurred. "I didn't know if I trusted Joe anymore, and I needed help. I didn't know what to do." I wiped my eyes. "But it seemed like God did, and He was talking to me through my writing."

My tone lightened, and I told them about going to church and then about my Miracle Day. "God told me to walk away from the past and love Joe unconditionally. He promised I would be okay and that we would have a new marriage.

"It didn't make sense, but God told me to love Joe back to health," I added. "It hasn't been easy, but I have forgiven him. Through our faith in God, we won."

Joe sat slumped in his chair, exhausted by his admissions. "I'm so, so sorry for what I did to your mom," he said. "I wish I could take it all back."

Casey and Tiffany came to me and wrapped their arms around my shoulders, murmuring words of comfort and disbelief. My shoulder grew damp with Tiffany's tears.

Joe quietly observed our embrace. With our confession, the final weight was lifted. No more secrets. Now I could be real with all of my girls.

Joe stood. "I'll go for a drive. Call me when you want me to come back."

I held up my hand in a sign of, "I love you."

He left the room.

"Why didn't you tell us?" Casey said. "Why didn't you let us help you?" Tears came to her eyes. She bent and hugged me again.

"I was afraid."

"Of what?" Tiffany sat beside me, rubbing my back.

"I was afraid you would tell me to leave. I wasn't strong enough to stay if you told me to leave him."

Following the face-to-face sessions with our four girls, we began our week of Skype meetings with the boys. We spoke with Conor and his wife, Tara, in Alaska. Joe and Conor had previously discussed the dangers of pornography, so Conor didn't seem too surprised to learn the rest of the story. Tara said that if they ever had marital problems she wanted to respond with love as I had.

Our final Skype session, on February 23, included Brendan, Sean, and Sean's fiancé, Mandy. When we finished sharing, Mandy said, "I wish I could give you guys a hug through Skype."

She got it. She understood what it took to save our marriage. Sean, in his quiet way, said he was glad we were still a family.

Brendan said he needed some time to think about all of this and decided not to communicate with his dad until he had time to reflect.

Joe shut down the computer. I gathered our papers and put them in the file drawer.

I couldn't believe the sense of freedom. "We did it, Joe. We're done." I clapped my hands.

"Yeah, but Brendan..."

"He said he needs time. He'll be okay."

"I guess." Joe sagged.

"Hey." I moved toward the stairs. "We need to celebrate."

"Where are you going?"

"I'll be right back." I ran up the stairs and found what I was looking for in the guestroom closet.

I carried two giant bubble wands downstairs.

Joe gave me a look. "Bubbles?"

"Yes. Let's go outside and celebrate."

"It's dark out."

I laughed, handing him a blue bubble wand. "You'd rather do this in the daylight? Besides there's a full moon. Come on."

He laughed, grabbed his coat off the chair, and followed me out the back door.

Like two small children, Joe and I ran around the yard holding out our bubble wands. A trail of bubbles streamed behind us. We turned and watched them bob and pop in the moonlight. A light breeze carried our creations into the darkness.

We waved our wands and bubbles floated, a testament to the lightening of our hearts and the freedom we'd been given.

I dipped my wand, raised it high, and spun, showering myself with bubbles. "I'm free, Joe. Isn't it amazing to be free?"

"Yes, it is, Babe." Joe nodded. "Now we're both free."

I wrote to our prayer warriors telling them we no longer carried the weight of our secrets.

Feedback from our prayer warriors:

"Amen. God is good. So glad for you both. I like the bubble exercise. Puff gone ....as far as the east is to the west. BLESSINGS AND JOY!"

"Wow! Fantastic news. A great example of being obedient to God to do the difficult stuff. We will continue to pray Ephesians 3:14-20 for you and your family, especially Joe's son to 'grasp how wide and long and high and deep is the love of Christ' (Ephesians 3:18)."

"Yay! Time to move forward and continue to grow in togetherness."

"Oh, thank you, Jesus. You are good and, oh, so faithful. Continue to bring healing and renewal to each member of this family. What an awesome testimony."

Telling the kids about Joe's betrayal and the two-year battle to save our marriage was one of the most frightening parts of our journey, but it was essential to my healing. If I had continued to carry Joe's secrets, my relationships with our kids would have remained superficial and one-sided, especially with the girls. Through the filter of my undisclosed sorrow, their joyful moments had become neutralized. When they spoke of their challenges, I had little to offer with my own life so out of control. Now I could share the strength and courage God had given me to fight for our marriage.

The initial reactions to our sharing were as varied as the personalities of our kids, but in time they were all glad we had been able to save our marriage and keep our family together.

A week after our Skype sessions, Brendan broke his silence and called Joe.

"Dad, it took some time, but I realize the good thing is that you two figured it out," Brendan said. "After all the times I've told you I messed things up, it was weird to hear you telling me that you had messed up, too."

The next time I saw Brendan, he pulled me aside to tell me how sorry he was that his dad put me through so much. His empathy for my pain meant the world to me.

Joe's admissions opened the door for honest discussions with his boys, where they now delve into issues that previously would have been off-limits. Joe shares what he wishes he had done differently both as a husband and a dad. The boys talk about their own doubts and insecurities. Joe hopes they will avoid some of the mistakes he made.

Recently, I asked the girls to reflect on their feelings. "For me, it wasn't about anger," Casey said. "I think the main feeling was shock because you two seemed perfect. It took a few months to think back through your visits, the vow renewal, and your church stuff before I was able to make all the connections to your story."

She continued, "When I thought more about it, I was relieved you had sheltered us from the emotional rollercoaster. Since you already forgave Joe, I didn't feel a need to make a judgment. It's your marriage. I chose not to make it about me."

In my conversation with Tiffany, she admitted she had been angry. "It wasn't fair that you had to go through that," Tiffany said. "I can't believe you came to my house that Christmas and I didn't even know you were crushed. I wish you had told me so I could have been there for you. I can't imagine how you stayed with him. I'm surprised you kept it secret for so long. You both faked it really well. You seemed like a happy, lovey-dovey couple."

Since then, Tiffany and I have had many in-depth conversations about forgiveness and the sad truths of objectification and sexual betrayal.

"How do you feel about it now?" I asked.

"Now, I don't think about it much. When I do, I'm impressed and dumbfounded that you still seem like a lovey-dovey couple."

Emily's relationship with Joe had always been strained. After hearing the truth, she carried residual anger toward him for years.

Thankfully, my prayers were answered recently when she and Joe decided to work on their relationship. They both realized that the tension between them was painful for me. Neither wanted to cause me anymore pain. I'm still surprised when they text each other instead of going through me.

Kelley and I have a comfortable relationship. She comes to me for advice, and when it is just the two of us, we often slip into deep soul-searching conversations.

I love being real with our kids. They know our marriage isn't perfect, but they see that it is richer because of our relationship with God and our honesty with each other.

Chapter 25

My Husband at College

The alarm went off at 5 a.m. I rolled out of bed and dressed for a run. The thermometer read forty-one degrees. My favorite running temperature.

I put in earbuds, slipped the head lamp over my ball cap, and stepped out the back door. The sky was clear, and I found Orion, twinkling brightly. A good indication of a beautiful day to come.

My early-morning runs were a time for contemplation and insight from the Lord. I turned on my iPod and fell into step with the music. My thoughts went straight to my habitual preoccupation, Joe and his journey. For the past two years, I'd tried to make him into the husband I wanted him to be, as if I owned him. That thought brought me up short—as if I owned him.

Joe didn't belong to me. He belonged to God. If anyone got to shape Joe, it was God. I could seek clarity and understanding about his journey. I could celebrate his successes, but I didn't own Joe. His journey wasn't mine to orchestrate. God gave me the gift of Joe as a companion to love and grow old with.

I worked on that idea while my music played in the background. The words of Danny Gokey's song, "Tell Your Heart to Beat Again," caught my attention. The lyrics told me to say goodbye to where I'd been. That's what I needed to do. I needed to say goodbye to two years of a broken heart. As the song suggested, love had pulled me through. God's love had pulled me through.

I had been trying to let go of Joe's past, meaning all the years of his brokenness. But I realized the past I should be saying goodbye to consisted of my two years of disclosure and grieving.

It was time to let those sad, broken memories fade. Joe could deal with his own past. I had plenty to worry about just letting go of mine.

***

Joe enjoyed being a full-time college student. The energy that used to go into triathlon training now went into schoolwork. He'd decided that with God's help, he would do his best to maintain an A average in his three-year physical therapy assistant program. He spent hours poring over his homework, and his first report card had come in with straight As.

I was grateful for Joe's excitement over a new career path but also felt threatened by the women in his classes and on campus.

One day I called my sister, Lorna, on my way to work. I just wanted to check in, but a half-hour later, I sat in the school parking lot crying.

"What do you mean he talks to you about the women in his classes?" Lorna was incredulous. "Why would he do that?"

"That's how I am helping him stay safe," I said. "He can't have secrets. He has to be transparent."

"Transparent? Right. He's being cruel." Lorna sighed. "You are trying to keep him safe, but what about you? Who is keeping you safe? Do you feel safe when he talks about his female classmates?"

"No, I hate it… but I'm afraid."

"What are you afraid of?"

"They do a lot of partner work in his physical therapy classes. I'm afraid if he doesn't talk about the women, he might fall into a relationship with one of them."

"Really? After all you guys have been through? I don't think so."

"I was so stupid before. I didn't pay attention."

"You told us that it's all in God's hands. Let Him take care of Joe."

I thought about that conversation all day. Lorna's words about keeping myself safe made sense. I'd become skittish. No matter how innocent the reference, each time Joe mentioned a woman's name it reignited fear, and my thoughts often ran with that fear.

Being enmeshed in Joe's sobriety wasn't good for me. If I stopped hearing about his female classmates, I might begin to focus on my own life, but I wanted an assurance that Joe would be safe if I let go of my vigilance.

Joe suggested we meet with his friend John Doyel, who also happened to be the founder of 180. I agreed, hoping his perspective would help.

The next evening, my stomach fluttered nervously on the drive to the restaurant. I couldn't shake the sense that my role in Joe's recovery was crucial. The thought of letting go frightened me.

John waved from a corner booth and stood. He greeted me, then turned to Joe. I stepped back and watched. John took Joe's offered hand and grasped his shoulder. Dressed in jeans and a dark button-down shirt, John stood taller than Joe. This man and the program he initiated had saved my husband and our marriage. The obvious warmth between the two men bolstered my sense that I could trust John's input.

The men moved apart, and we slid into the booth.

John gestured toward me. "So, tell me why we're here."

"Okay." I slipped out of my coat. "I'm proud of how far Joe has come, but I'm nervous about the women in his classes. I'm afraid he might slip if he doesn't talk to me about them. The problem is, I don't think it's good for me."

"Give me an example," John said.

"Well, yesterday Joe told me he joked with Brittany about putting his hair in a French braid. He wanted to have the same hair style as Sandy and Crissy who sit in his row."

"We were just joking around," Joe said. "I wanted to share with Hil because it was funny."

John looked at me. "Did you think it was funny?"

I shook my head. "No."

John turned to Joe. "She doesn't think it's funny."

"But it was funny." Joe insisted, gesturing with his hands. "That's what I'm trying to explain—"

"Joe," John said sharply. "Hilarie doesn't think it's funny. That means it's not funny."

Joe's animation deflated. "Oh." He slumped and turned to me. "I'm sorry, Babe. I wasn't hearing you."

I looked into his warm, blue eyes and believed him. I knew he didn't want to hurt me. He wanted me to heal, but he just didn't get it. *Why can't he understand how fragile I am? I'm afraid of other women. I don't want them to like him or think he's funny. I don't even want them to talk to Joe or him talk to them.*

"Okay, let's get this straightened out." John focused his attention on Joe. "Before you do anything, I want you to stop and consider how it will make your wife feel. Really think about it. You'll be surprised how that will change your behavior. Your job is to guard your wife's heart. Do that, and you will both be safe."

Joe nodded. "I can do that."

John stretched and put his hands behind his head. "What else do you need from me?"

"I want Joe to stop talking to me about his female classmates unless, of course, he's in danger. Is that okay?"

"Are you asking me if Joe will still be safe if you back off?"

"Yes."

"Definitely," John said. "I've known Joe for—what's it been, a year, right?"

"Almost a year and a half," Joe said.

"I see this guy every week and I hear his heart. He is working hard and, besides, any idea you have about keeping him safe is an illusion. Joe has to make that decision himself. His small group will help him with anything that could be dangerous for his sobriety. He'll let you know if he's struggling. You guys are in good shape."

"But I feel like God is telling me to help Joe."

"I'm sure He is." John chuckled. "But not through vigilance. Stop watching Joe so closely. He's doing what he needs to."

"Then what am I supposed to do?"

"Hear him, love him, support him."

"So just stay quiet." I crossed my arms over my chest.

"Absolutely not. But if he tells you about his struggles, praise him for talking about it. Listen and let him work through it. It's really hard for us to admit our weaknesses, especially to our wives."

I relaxed. "You mean, hear the love in your husband's disclosures."

"Yeah, I like that."

"Those are God's words, not mine."

"Smart guy."

John still hadn't addressed my concern. "What about my feelings?"

"You need to be honest about your feelings, also. Just don't beat him up. We already beat ourselves up enough." He and Joe shared a glance.

Driving home from the restaurant, I had a better sense of my place in Joe's recovery. Supporting him wasn't about monitoring his behavior or about him sharing every detail of his day. Being supportive required that I trust Joe's commitment to me and our marriage, listen to his heart, and cheer him on when he made progress. Joe knew how to keep himself safe, and the guys would help him. I needed to give him space to establish new patterns for interacting with people.

I also needed to believe in the work God was doing in his heart. I wanted to re-establish a friendship and marriage based on trust.

The next day Joe and I read through our contract. We crossed out a few of his transparency requirements that began, "I will tell Hilarie when…." We initialed and dated the changes.

I felt like I had scaled a mountain and now stood at the summit. The clouds parted, and the view was promising. I inhaled the fresh air of hope and attempted once more, to close the lid on my dumpster.

Sadly, the intense fear I had lived with for more than two years ran deep.

A conversation with God through my hands:
Saturday, April 2, 2016
God: *Baby Girl, I understand your fear, but I don't know if you understand it yet. What are you afraid of? I am here in your heart. I have a plan for you and still you are afraid. You know I will never leave you, that I have always taken care of you. You feel My love and still you are afraid. Why is My love not enough for you?*

Me: *I ask myself that question and the answer is hard to find. Could it be that I still expect Joe to be perfect? I can't accept that he is human, that he cannot give me what You give me. He will never be the idol I made him out to be. I see him differently, with an awareness that he is just a man. He is imperfect. He has a brokenness that will never go away. But You are in his heart. What am I afraid of if I understand that? The worst has already happened. He got lost in an affair, and I got lost in the horror of the truth. I think that's what I am afraid of, Lord. I am afraid of losing myself again. When I am triggered, I have a deep fear of being lost.*

God: *Good, Baby Girl. What is that fear? What are you afraid will happen?*

Me: *I am afraid attention from other women will spark Joe's desire to be admired, to be seen as big and strong and manly. I am afraid he will want more of that. Even if he can resist, his desire for admiration from women frightens me.*

God: *Why?*

Me: *Because it makes me less. I feel like I am not important. I was never jealous before. Now I am, and it is painful. I don't want anyone to give Joe attention because I don't want him to enjoy it. Any attention from a woman can be dangerous. It might feed his ego and leave him wanting more. The attention could breed discontent with the woman he has at home—me. I used to be proud that women liked my husband. I guess that fed my ego.*

I'm not answering the question. What am I afraid of?

I am afraid of putting my trust back in this man you have given me. I am afraid of falling again. I was so lost, Lord. I didn't know who I was anymore. That's it. The fear came from not knowing who I was. Maybe I'm not afraid of losing Joe as much as I'm afraid of losing myself.

I remember loving my life. I was walking in the sunshine, proud of who we were. Then Joe shoved me into a nightmare, and I got lost.

You rescued me. You handed me my computer and said, "Write, Baby Girl. Write so I can find you."

What am I afraid of? I am afraid of being Alice in the looking glass with no idea who I am. I am afraid of something that doesn't exist anymore. The nightmare is over. I will never be lost and helpless again because I have You. You have led me every step of the way. And...

And you gave me Joe. You gave me a man who was strong even in his shame. You gave me the gift of this man, not so he would hurt me, but so we could bring each other to You. That awful December night, Joe dragged me into his darkness. Together, we made the long journey toward Your light. You wanted both of us to find You, and through our shared pain, we did. We were lost and broken. Then we reached out and grabbed on to the hand that had always been there waiting for us.

I don't need to be afraid. I will never get lost again even if Joe does. I don't have to be afraid because You are near. Who I am belongs to You. I am Your Baby Girl, and You will always show me the way.

Chapter 26

Support Groups

Joe and I mistakenly believed the new 180 support group would begin at Delaware Grace shortly after we told our kids, with Hope and Healing to follow in the spring. We had not yet learned that things happen in God's time, not ours. In our enthusiasm as new believers, we couldn't understand why church leadership was reluctant to let us start these challenging ministries.

Discussions about Hope and Healing began in early April. Cathy, whom I'd grown close to after the women's retreat, would co-lead the group. She had been involved with various Delaware Grace ministries over the years and had a solid knowledge of the Bible. We believed we were ready, but no one would give us a start date for the ministries.

By mid-April, Joe was frustrated. One of the elders questioned his ability to lead the group despite the fact that Joe had been leading a small group at Vineyard for months.

One Sunday evening, Joe and I sat on the couch watching a movie. The wife onscreen stood over her husband. He sat with his head clasped in his hands, the pain of regret etched in his posture.

"It's over, Ben," she said. "I can't take any more of your cheating. I'm filing for divorce."

Joe paused the movie. We stared at the frozen screen, each of us lost in thoughts of how easily our story could have gone that way.

"It wasn't until I almost lost you," Joe said, "that I realized you and our marriage are the only things that matter. We have history and love that goes deeper than anything I could get from someone else. Everything I experienced with other women was shallow and unsatisfying."

I pulled my feet up under me. "But they gave you things I couldn't give you."

"Yeah, but it wasn't real. The interactions I had were all two-dimensional fantasy. I was just too stupid to see that. You give me so much more. Our relationship is real. That's what I want, the true intimacy I can only have with you."

Later, when we climbed into bed, Joe's words came back to me and kept me from sleeping. Instead of focusing on the intimacy he wanted, my thoughts turned toward his past fantasy life. I got out of bed, anxious to chase away the negative thoughts.

It had snowed all day, a late April snow. I put on my coat and boots and stepped outside into the beautiful night. The thoughts followed me. *Other women gave him things you couldn't. You weren't good enough.*

I pushed away the lies and called on God, asking Him to move my thoughts to a better place. I waited patiently, standing still in the snow. The fresh, chilly air numbed my cheeks and cleared my thoughts.

Truth began to settle into my heart. *Any woman can make Joe feel like a man. I am the only one who makes him feel loved.*

I smiled and allowed the wisdom of those thoughts to seep into my understanding. My mind regained balance. I circled the house, kicking up icy crystals, enjoying their sparkle in the moonlight. *Any woman can feed Joe's ego. I am the only one who can love him the way I do.*

I heard God add, *Just like Me.* I went back in the house to write.

A conversation with God through my hands.
Sunday, April 17, 2016

God: *Just like My love for you.*

Me: *Is there more?*

God: *Baby Girl, I love you so deeply and so consistently that nothing can compare. I have loved you since the beginning of time. Don't you see? You could have come to Me at any point with your hurts and worries. I would have poured My love and Holy Spirit onto you. I would have given you peace when you needed it most. I would have comforted you and helped you see that I work all things for good.*

Me: *This isn't flowing easily from my fingers. I think there may be something more, something that I am not getting. Lord, I feel like You have more for me, a deeper message.*

God: *When My children choose anything but Me to fill a need, it is called sin. My son died so you would come to Me. When you were a young woman, you fed your ego through a job, accomplishments, your children. Now, you hope to define yourself by this new ministry. You are looking for a mirror to tell you things you wish to hear. That's why you are stumbling over getting it started. This group is not about you, Baby Girl. It is for My glory. What pulls you away from Me, Baby Girl? Think, think—what do you want to see in your mirror?*

Me: *I don't know. I'm not sure what I'm looking for... Oh, I know. I want to be seen as organized, wise, competent, creative, insightful.*

God: *Yes, yes. You want this group to be a mirror of those things. Baby Girl, you will not fulfill My purpose if you are looking for something beyond a relationship with Me. You will not benefit from My love for you unless you look to Me to meet your needs.*

You want to be seen as competent? Ask for My guidance.

You want to be seen as organized? Trust Me to lead you.

You want to be seen as wise? Baby Girl, you are up at this hour talking to Me and listening. You are so wise. But that should not feed your ego. The ego is not part of My relationship with you. You are only as wise as you are able to come to Me.

Let Me be your mirror, Baby Girl. Let Me show you all that you are and all that you can be. When you tap into the plan I have for you, you become My daughter. You become a sister to My Son. Hold out your hand and clasp the hand of My Son, the only perfect man. He is Me, Baby Girl. When you look to Me, I am your husband, your lover, your best friend, and there is no betrayal.

I want all of My children to walk with Me in the light, free of sin. I want to be your mirror. Look at Me to see the amazing woman you are. I am in you. I shine through you into the darkness in this world. Think of Me and My love shines through you. No pride, no ego, just love.

Let Me be your mirror. Then point others to Me so they can see who they really are, in the light of My love. This is about you and Me, Baby Girl, not about you and your husband. You are My bride and I will never leave you. I will always cherish you. You are My Baby Girl.

Me: *I will look to You to be my mirror, Lord. I won't need to build myself up in other people's eyes because I know who I am in Yours.*

***

I wanted to use Meg Wilson's book, *Hope After Betrayal*, with my group. Her book stood out from others I'd read. She and her husband survived this journey when she learned to look to God for direction. Her book taught me to identify Satan's lies and replace them with truth that comes only from God.

I emailed her administrative assistant to ask about ordering multiple copies of the book and workbook. She suggested I speak directly with Meg, whose current mission was to help women start ministries like the one she led in Vancouver, Washington.

I almost politely declined the offer. I didn't want to bother her. I couldn't imagine she would be interested in talking to me. Then I remembered that God was in charge and He wanted me to put up sails.

I took a deep breath and said, "Thank you. That would be great."

The next day, my stomach fluttered with nervous excitement as I waited for Meg's 1 p.m. call. I set a pad and pen by the phone. I didn't want to forget anything she said in my excitement over speaking with a woman who might become a mentor.

When the phone rang, I hesitated only a moment before picking it up.

Meg's energy and enthusiasm for her ministry was evident throughout our conversation. Thrilled that I planned to use her book, she offered to send her facilitator guide that was still in rough draft form and a DVD that would introduce each chapter. We talked for an hour. Her words were infused with a love of God and faith in His truths.

When I hung up, I was energized and ready to move forward.

Our small Hope and Healing committee decided to announce the plan for our support group at the women's Bible study potluck. I agreed to share my testimony as way of introduction.

My body hummed with anticipation as I drove to the address I had been given. I knew some of the women in the group and wondered what they would think of me after hearing my story. Would they avoid me? Would they hate Joe? It didn't matter. God called me to this ministry, and I trusted His plan. This was for His glory, not my popularity.

I pulled up in front of a cute ranch style home and followed a group of women into the house. Our host greeted me warmly and invited me to share in their meal.

After dinner and social time, dishes were cleared, and everyone gathered. I stood and walked to the front of the room, feeling like I was dreaming. I couldn't believe I was actually going to use my story to help other women.

I began to read, distantly aware of the tremor in my voice. "When Joe and I first came to Delaware Grace two years ago, we were very lost. My husband was filled with shame and remorse, and I was a walking ball of fear and pain."

I paused and wondered if anyone in the room would identify with my experience.

"On December 23, two years ago, I picked up my husband's phone, and life as I knew it changed forever. My world came crashing down when I realized he was having an affair. In that moment, everything I believed about my life and myself disappeared…."

I spoke of the nightmare I'd lived through and the loneliness of that time.

"We came to church as non-believers," I said. "Pastor Frank caught my attention that first morning when he said, 'No perfect people here.' His words gave me hope that we might be in the right place."

As I told my story, some of the ladies nodded. A young woman in the back of the room held a tissue to her eyes.

"Our story continues with two people who have found Jesus Christ and a marriage that survived one of life's worst challenges." Then I spoke of the support we found at the Vineyard Church through 180 and Hearts Restored.

I closed with an announcement that Delaware Grace Church planned to offer similar support through Hope and Healing and 180 Men's Ministry. There would be fliers in the church lobby once we started.

The women applauded when I finished speaking. I felt both elated and relieved that it was over. I did it. God told me to share with the ladies, and I did.

Several women approached me afterward, praising God's glory in my marriage and thanking me for my testimony. Flushed with euphoria, I accepted their hugs and kind words of affirmation, stating that it was all for God's glory.

The gathering ended shortly after my talk. Women collected their potluck dishes and coats. I scanned the thinning group looking for the tearful woman I'd noticed while speaking. I had hoped to talk with her, but she was gone.

On the way home, the euphoria faded, and Satan crept onto my shoulder with his lies. Not one of the women I spoke with gave any indication they might join Hope and Healing. *I must have failed. I said the wrong things. My testimony wasn't good enough. Whatever made me think I could do this?*

I shoved Satan and his lies off my shoulder.

None of this was about me. I would carry no pride or attachment to the outcome. I did my part. I shared my story as I believed God wanted me to. The rest would happen in His time, not mine.

With that, I turned on Christian music and enjoyed the beautiful ride home.

***

And then, of course, temptations continued to challenge both of us. One evening while making a purchase from an attractive woman, Joe felt the old desires stir. He wanted to continue the banter and fuel his ego with her attention, but instead, he left quickly and rushed home to tell me about the incident.

Thursday, May 5, 2016

I'm here to ask for help, God. Joe was tempted tonight. He told me about it so it wouldn't feel like a secret. Help me let it go. Joe was right to tell me the truth, and he didn't do anything wrong. He was just tempted.

I'm pulled back to thoughts of how easily he betrayed me all those years, but he did not betray me this time. Help me honor the love in his disclosure. Help me walk away from this episode and leave it with You, so I can get some sleep.

There is nothing I can do about his temptations. Nothing. All I can do is choose how I will respond when he tells me about them. Please, Lord, let me respond with Your grace and love. Help me to say and mean these words. "I love you, Joe. I am proud of you for maintaining your sobriety in a tough situation. I am grateful for your commitment to integrity. Thank you for trusting me with the truth. I feel loved and cherished. I believe in you."

Thank You for giving me the power of Your spirit, Lord, so I can believe those words. I'm going to bed.

On my run the next day, I thought about Eve in the Garden of Eden and her response to temptation. Everything she needed was available to her, but Satan's deceitful words bred a desire for the fruit she could not have. Satan put doubt and justification in Eve's heart. She bought the lies, fell, and took Adam with her. "The woman saw that the fruit of the tree was good for food and pleasing to the eye … she took some and ate it. She also gave some to her husband, who was with her, and he ate it" (Genesis 3:6).

I did not want to be that Eve to my Adam. I wanted to learn from her mistake. When Joe spoke about the temptation that pulled at him, he was shaken. He wanted to diffuse the enemy's power by sharing his upsetting experience with me. I heard the love in his disclosure, his desire to be a better man.

I was tempted to get angry, cry, or distance myself. I didn't want him to feel the pull of lust that an attractive woman created. I wanted to lash out because Satan tried to pull him off course. I wanted to blame my husband, to talk him out of his feelings. I wanted to jump up and down, to scream and yell, to make it all go away.

It wouldn't have taken much to break Joe's fragile attempt to trust me with the truth. Secrets are the enemy's foothold, but truth can be painful and scary.

I was a new Eve to my Adam, and I just listened and loved him.

Chapter 27

Innocent Love

With school out for the summer, I flew to New Jersey for an extended visit with Casey. Joe planned to drive out later in the week. Casey and I spent the entire first day together with no burden of secrets between us.

On my way up to the guest room for the night, she handed me something she had written and asked if I would read it when I had a chance. I got into my pajamas, turned on the bedside lamp, and climbed under the blanket. Nestled in the quiet room, I picked up Casey's writing.

She wrote of her love for her husband. Her words brought tears to my eyes. She trusted her man to keep her safe, to love and cherish her always. My tears spilled over as I read. Theirs was the beautiful, innocent love that dreams are made of. How blessed my little girl was to experience that love for her husband. I reached for the tissues beside the bed and wiped at my cheeks. I cried with gratitude that she had found that precious love with her husband. I also cried because I had lost it.

I finished reading, dried my eyes, and lay still, thinking of how my experience had redefined my perception of love. Was it possible that my loss brought something better?

When I woke the next morning, I put it all together.

Sunday, June 27, 2016

God, You gave me the gift of innocent love for Joe, and I held on to it for twelve years. I felt lucky, as though I had done something to deserve this special man. Then the nightmare came and now the healing.

This morning I realize innocent love is how You want us to love You. You want to be our best friend, the one we run to in times of trouble. You want us to feel safe and cherished wrapped in Your loving arms.

With You I will always be safe. If I come to You with all my worries, You will gladly take them from me. If I trust You, I will be joyful and peaceful the rest of my days. Lord, You want us to feel about You the way Casey feels about her husband. You want to be with us in all our moments. You want to comfort us when we are sad and fearful and celebrate with us when we are joyful.

Lord, what if You gave me that innocent love for Joe not so I would lose it, but so I would look to You for more? You created my innocence because You want me to come to You as a child runs to her father. You gave me that naïve love so one day I might love You the same way. You wanted my heart.

Then what about Joe? That's the amazing part. Joe really is Your blessing in my life. Through him, You taught me to love deeply, to forgive fully, to have patience and empathy. You love me in the deepest parts of my heart, while Joe loves me closer to the surface. He is Your blessing, Your gift to me. But he is also my life lesson. He is teaching me to rely on You.

When Joe found me fourteen years ago, I'd been hurt and would not allow myself to be vulnerable with anyone. Loving another man was not part of my plan. I planned to love my girls and figure everything out on my own. You didn't want that for me. You didn't want me to live a life of isolation.

You wanted me to learn to love a man, then learn to love You, and now learn to love other people. You broke into my hardened heart with Joe. I fell into a deep, all-consuming love. When I was shattered, You gently awakened my heart again so I could fall in love with You.

***

Casey was busy the next afternoon, so I went for a long bike ride, exploring the neighborhoods that surrounded her town. Many of the streets were busy with traffic, so my mission was to find the less congested roads.

About eight miles into my ride I pedaled up a long, quiet hill in a wooded area, just as my phone rang. At the next level stretch, I stopped and saw the call was from Joe. He had also texted saying he wanted to talk when I was available.

The message seemed urgent and the road was quiet, so I called him back.

After a short greeting, Joe said, "I have to tell you something you won't want to hear."

My heart thudded in my chest. "Okay, I'm ready," I said evenly.

"Last night I almost contacted Cindy. I didn't, but I came close. It scared me."

"Oh…" I managed.

"I'm okay now, and I'll be driving out to New Jersey tomorrow to be with you."

"Did you contact one of your guys?" I asked quietly.

Joe hesitated. "Not right away. I called them later."

I wanted to throw my bike into the woods, sit on the curb, and cry. I quieted myself and said, "If you didn't want to call them, why didn't you call me?"

"I don't know."

I heard defeat in his voice. He had beat the temptation, but now he deflated knowing that he'd let me down. I lay my bike gently against the curb and sat beside it.

"I have one question. Is there anything else you need to put in the dumpster?"

"No," he said. "That's it."

"Okay, you won the battle," I said with more confidence than I felt. "Now you're telling me about it. That's a win-win." I kept my tone light. "What could you do next time to keep yourself safe?"

Joe's voice brightened. "I should have contacted someone the minute she came to mind."

He knew what he needed to do to keep himself safe. The difficult part was to make those choices when it was hardest to do so.

Emotionally drained, I climbed on my bike and made my way back to Casey's house. By the time I arrived, I had recovered.

"How was your ride?" Casey said.

"I'd say it was successful."

It surprised me that I felt balanced. Each time Joe shared a difficult truth, I seemed to recover more quickly.

The next morning, I woke before daylight. My first thought was of my phone conversation with Joe.

I pulled my computer into my lap.

Tuesday, June 28, 2016

Joe was severely tempted last night, Lord. I guess when we are apart there will be a strong possibility of an attack. I have been fearful of temptations, but you know what? That doesn't scare me as much anymore. This morning I realize I am much more afraid of secrets. A secret is the only thing that has the power to destroy our marriage.

Joe and I have felt secure and safe these days. He is strong in his faith and his commitment to sobriety. I have been winning my battle with triggers. After two and a half years, life is starting to seem normal. But whenever the world is most sweet, the enemy will look for a way to attack.

I guess these attacks are the "thorn in my flesh," a message that I should not become too confident. Although I have prayed for temptation and triggers to be removed, You have said, "My grace is sufficient for you, for My power is made perfect in weakness" (2 Corinthians 12:7). This battle will never be far from us. Knowing that will ensure that we keep You close, so You can keep us strong.

You are using temptation to help Joe understand he can never get lazy. He can't let his guard down or Satan will try to win him back. Temptation will be a thorn in both of our sides. We can't become complacent about the gift You have given us in each other. Our love is both solid and fragile. It appears that nothing can tear us apart, and yet there is something so small it could shred us to pieces.

Not temptation. Not even a slip or a fall. The thing that could destroy our marriage is a secret. A secret is small like a thorn. A thorn will irritate, then fester and infect, becoming a danger to the flesh surrounding it. A tiny thorn could cause an entire limb to become useless with swelling and pain.

A secret has destructive power. One little secret left untold would quickly fester and spread into the healthy tissue of our marriage. The lie that Satan continues to tempt Joe with is, "No one will know." True, there would be no evidence of a slip. Joe knows the tricks of deceit, and I am very trusting.

So, the only thing left in the wake of a slip would be one tiny secret and an omission or two to cover it up. Oh, that's right, omissions are lies. The enemy wants us to forget that.

Okay, so there would be one tiny secret and...

Well, one big secret and a few lies of omission.... That isn't quite true, either.

One big secret, some lies of omission, some bigger lies when responding to direct questions, some internal justifications, and a blocked discussion with God.

Come on, it was just one tiny slip. Can't a guy have a bad day?

Really? One slip. It will never happen again.

If I tell her, it will break her heart and ruin her day. I can keep it to myself just this once.

If it happens again, then I will definitely say something. I promised I would tell, and I will, but it can wait. I won't slip again.

Oh, what about my accountability guys? They think I'm the poster child for fidelity. I'm a leader. I can't let them down. Just one little slip. They slip all the time. I'm not going to say anything tonight. I want to chew on it a bit. I'll tell them next week.

I'll talk to God tomorrow.

I'll read my Bible later.

The secret festered, and Satan smiled, believing the new 180 group would be his next playground.

I closed my laptop and sat back against the pillows. *Wow. Where did that come from?* I laughed to myself knowing exactly where it came from. God was helping me get well. Listening to Him made me stronger.

The early-morning sun shone through the blinds. I noticed my Bible lying on the suitcase, and I thought of my recent reading about Job.

Job was a wealthy, respected, God-loving man. Through no fault of his own, he lost everything. Understandably, Job's grief weighed heavily on him. With time he remembered God's plan was bigger than his personal pain. Rather than wallow in sorrow, he chose to trust God. His faith was rewarded, and over time his wealth was restored more abundantly than before.

Elation swept through me as I drew a parallel between my situation and Job's. My life was like his. None of this was what I expected when I moved into our beautiful log home with my big, strong Marine who promised to love and protect me.

Through no fault of my own, I lost everything. My dreams for our marriage were trampled by the reality of Joe's betrayal, but God didn't want me to wallow over the past. Like Job, He wanted me to be a testament to the beauty He brings from the ashes of tragedy. This wasn't what I signed up for, but maybe I'd end up with something better.

I shook my head, amazed at the crazy new way my thoughts ran. If someone had told me three years earlier that one day, I'd lie in bed thinking about the Bible, I would have thought they were delusional. Now, God was with me all the time, and each day He gave me the strength and understanding I needed to face the next challenge. Joe wasn't the only one who had changed for the better. What an incredible journey.

I stretched contentedly, then jumped out of bed, ready to face the amazing day God had planned, just for me.

***

Back in Ohio, on July 13, my sixtieth birthday began with delicious chocolate chip pancakes cooked by my wonderful husband. We had planned a quiet day: a bike ride, a picnic lunch, and a women's meeting at Vineyard later that evening.

Our breakfast conversation started with a discussion of possible bike riding destinations, then moved to our confusion over our delayed ministries. For seven months we had tried to start support groups at Delaware Grace. Had we misunderstood? Did God have a different plan for us?

Joe's phone rang. He picked it up, and his face lit with a smile. He put one hand over the receiver. Pastor Frank wanted to know when we might be available for a meeting.

I tapped on my wrist and said, "Now." There could only be one reason for Frank to meet with us, our ministries.

We climbed into the car.

"Wouldn't this be an awesome birthday present?" I said.

Joe nodded, grinning.

We were quiet on the drive to church, afraid to voice our excitement in case this was another false alarm. Every now and then we looked at each other and giggled, our anticipation bubbling over.

The meeting didn't last long. Pastor Frank began with an apology about how long it had taken to give us an answer about the groups. He leaned back in his chair with a big grin across his face.

"We met yesterday and made a decision," Pastor Frank said. "If you two feel God is calling you to these ministries, we will trust Him to make it happen."

Joe and I looked at each other. Our mouths hung open.

"Really?" I couldn't believe it.

Pastor Frank gave me a thumbs-up and a nod.

"Yay!" I clapped, then brought my clenched hands to my mouth. My eyes teared up. The waiting was over.

My breath caught when I realized it was Wednesday. "We plan to meet on Thursdays," I said. "Can Hope and Healing start tomorrow?"

"Yes." He chuckled. "With our blessings. Thank you both for what you are doing."

What a perfect birthday present. I chattered all the way home about the book we were going to use, and the things Meg Wilson had told me about leading a group.

That evening, the ladies at Vineyard Church congratulated me on the news about Hope and Healing and prayed with me over the women who might come to the group.

During our time together, a heavy storm swept through the area. The skies turned black, and I wondered if we might have trouble getting home. Thankfully the storm passed before our meeting broke up.

I sang worship songs all the way home, praising God for an amazing sixtieth birthday.

When I pulled into the driveway, Joe stood in the front yard—and I couldn't see our house.

I leapt out of the car, my heart pounding, confused by what I saw. Much of the ancient maple tree that used to tower over our house now lay on the ground completely hiding our home.

Joe smiled. "Didn't even touch the house," he called out and motioned for me to follow him. "There's more."

We walked to what had been a gigantic tree with several huge limbs. Joe helped me climb onto the largest limb which now lay at the base of the trunk. From that vantage point, I could see the tree ran the full fifty feet along the front of our house. Only one small branch leaned on the porch.

"Look back here." Joe pointed toward the back of the house.

I maneuvered carefully and saw another giant limb had fallen at a ninety-degree angle to the first. The limb just missed the side of the house and the deck.

God's power of protection brought us safely through another storm.

The following evening, a vivid rainbow stretched across the sky beckoning me to Delaware Grace Church.

I entered the large meeting room and looked around, wondering how to make a cozy space for our small group. I set up a table in the corner, placed four chairs around it, and put a box of tissues in the center.

Two women joined me that evening. We huddled around my small Bluetooth speaker and sang "Holy Spirit," by Francesca Battistelli. The music and our tentative voices filled the huge room. When the song ended, the melody lingered.

I briefly shared my story, then invited the ladies to speak. With tears, Anna spoke of her shattered dreams and the lies that continued to break her heart.

Patty handed tissues across the table, then talked about the agony of her discovery and the loneliness she felt. She said that God found her in the darkness and eased her sorrow. On good days she remembered to have faith in His plan. One day He would make all things new.

The women ministered to each other's wounds as only fellow travelers can do.

I felt a nudge to remain quiet. It confused me. I had waited so long for the opportunity to use Our Life Lesson for good, but this wasn't about me, and it wasn't about imparting wisdom. I had no magic words to bring healing.

My job was to provide a place where women could find comfort in each other and grow closer to God in the process. A place where they could find … Hope and Healing.

Epilogue

On Christmas morning, three years after Our Life Lesson began, Joe and I sat on the couch wearing matching red and black plaid pajamas. It had been a chaotic couple of days. All seven of our children and their families were home for the holiday—the first time we'd had them all together in eight years. They came because they loved us, imperfect marriage and all.

I watched our grandchildren tear the wrapping paper off their gifts. Tiffany's oldest, Tommy, jumped up. "Thank you, thank you! I love it." He ran to us, and Joe scooped him up for a quick tickle.

Casey came into the room and placed her precious little girl in my arms. Joe leaned in to kiss the baby's forehead. Her eyes lit. She giggled and grabbed at his beard.

I looked around the room at our busy family, talking and laughing together. Joy filled my heart. God had worked a miracle. He helped me stay and love Joe, even when it didn't make sense.

"We made it, Joe," I said quietly. "We're still a family."

Joe nodded. "We sure are, Babe."

With eyes glistening, he kissed the top of my head and pulled me close.

For I know the plans I have for you," declares the LORD, "plans to prosper you and not to harm you, plans to give you hope and a future. (Jeremiah 29:11)

Photos

1. The best Christmas ever! (December 25, 2016)

2. Joe graduates summa cum laude as a physical therapist assistant. (May 2017)

3. Yes, that is me finishing the Columbus Marathon. (October 16, 2016)

4. Our amazing kids. Back: Brendan, Sean, Conor. Front: Kelley, Joe, me, Emily, Casey and Tiffany. All together again in Outer Banks North Carolina, along with four spouses, one fiancé, and ten grandchildren. (June 2019)

A Bit More About My Journey

As you might imagine, there were other significant events during the season of our Life Lesson. Some were heart crushing experiences, best left in the fading past, but others were quite joyous, and I want to share some of those with you.

During the ten months from August 2015 to June 2016, Joe and I were blessed with four new grandchildren. The Christmas of 2016 from my epilogue was truly a festive time with five big cousins running through the house, three toddlers waddling in the sunroom and the baby being passed around. Joe and I were quite aware of how different that Christmas might have been had God not intervened with his lessons of unconditional love.

Other notable events following the summer of my sixtieth birthday were my completion of the Ohio Half Ironman in late August 2016 and two months later, the Columbus Marathon. Sadly, Joe had last-minute health issues that kept him from joining me at the starting gates, but God used my solo experiences as a challenge meant to rebuild my damaged self-esteem.

The following spring, May 2017, Joe graduated summa cum laude from his physical therapy assistant program. He now supports physical healing for patients at local facilities and teaches at the college he had attended.

That summer, I embarked on a journey to becoming a Christian writer.

My writer's journey

In June of 2016, I believed that God wanted me to turn my journaling into a book. For six months I poured over approximately 725 single-spaced typed pages from that difficult three-year period. That January 2018, I finished editing my journals—my book was complete. I showed my work to an editor friend who told me outright, "This is great material for a book, but it is not a book." I left our meeting in tears. One of her many suggestions was to turn my journal into a memoir. When I got home, I googled, "What is a memoir?"

At the advice of my author friend, Meg Wilson, I registered for a writers' conference. A month later, as I drove through the gates of the Billy Graham Training Center, for the Asheville Christian Writers Conference, I wondered, *Who is Billy Graham?* I had much to learn on many levels. During that busy conference weekend, I met with a writing coach, Larry Leech. He read my first chapter, which had been rewritten in my best attempt at a memoir, and said, "I want to help you write this book."

I spent the rest of the conference discovering how much I didn't know about writing. At home, I threw myself into learning all I could about narration, scenes and dialogue. No longer obsessed with Joe and our healing journey, I now spent the winter obsessed with writing. I wrote and rewrote the first thirty pages of what had once been my journal, until I felt like I understood at least a little about writing.

That May 2018, I hired Larry to teach me what books and podcasts could not. Through his emailed comments, I learned of both the frustrations and the value of constructive criticism. At times, our hour-long phone sessions were like therapy, where Larry encouraged me to revisit the fear and anger accompanying Joe's betrayal, so I could spill those emotions onto the page. I grew as a writer, learning, grieving, editing, and rewriting. It was all part of the journey.

The following winter, I went back to the Billy Graham Training Center and the Asheville Christian Writers Conference with my book. *We Survived Infidelity* won the conference book contest, giving me the confidence to press on to publication another year later.

It is easy to see that God had a plan all along with the ministries that Joe and I now lead, the significant changes we've each made personally and all of the blessings we've experienced during and since our life lesson. God intended to bring much joy and purpose from our trials. And now through this book, we've been given an opportunity to use our story for His glory. What an awesome God!

Notes

Chapter 6
Bercht, Ann. *My Husband's Affair Became the Best Thing that Ever Happened to Me*. Victoria, Canada: Trafford Publishing, 2004.

Chapter 9
Beattie, Melody. *Beyond Codependency: And getting better all the time*. USA: Hazelden, 1988.

Chapter 10
Glass, Shirley P. *Not "Just Friends:" Rebuilding Trust and Recovering Your Sanity After Infidelity*. New York: Free Press, 2003.

Nelson, Portia. "Autobiography in Five Short Chapters." *There's a Hole in My Sidewalk*. New York and Oregon: Atria and Beyond Words, 2018, Originally published 1977.

Chapter 11
Young, William. *The Shack*. Newbury Park, CA: Windblown Media, 2007.

Chapter 12
Beattie, Melody. *The Language of Letting Go: Daily Meditations on Codependency*. USA: Hazelden, 1990.

Chapter 13
Dyer, Wayne. *Ten Secrets for Success and Inner Peace*. California: Hay House Inc. 2016.

Jarrard, John, Lisa Palas, and Will Robinson. "There's No Way." *40-hour Week*, Alabama, 1985.

Chapter 14
Steffens, Barbara and Means, Marsha. *Your Sexually Addicted Spouse: How Partners Can Cope and Heal*. Far Hills, NJ: New Horizon Press, 2009.

Chapter 15
Story, Laura. "Blessings." *Blessings*, Laura Story, 2011.

Chapter 16
Ortberg, John. *If You Want to Walk on Water You've Got to Get Out of the Boat*. Grand Rapids: Zondervan, 2014.

Chapter 19
Katie, Byron. *Loving What Is*. New York: Harmony Books, 2003.

Chapter 20
Means, Marsha. *Journey to Healing and Joy*. Createspace, 2014.

Perkins, Bill. *When Good Men are Tempted*. Grand Rapids: Zondervan, 2007.

Getty, Keith and Townsend, Stuart. "Speak, O Lord." Thank You Music, 2005.

Chapter 22
Markova, Dawna. *I Will Not Die an Unlived Life*. Berkeley, CA: Conari Press, 2000.

Chapter 25
Gokey, Danny. "Tell Your Heart to Beat Again." *Hope in Front of Me*, 2014.

Chapter 26
Wilson, Meg. *Hope After Betrayal*. Grand Rapids: Kregel Publications, 2007.

Chapter 27
Battistelli, Francesca. "Holy Spirit." *If We're Honest*, 2014.

OTHER RESOURCES

Allen, Susan. *The Healing Choice Guidebook*. Colorado Springs: Waterbrook Press, 2008.

Arterburn, Stephen and Martinkus, Jason B. *Worthy of Her Trust: What you need to do to rebuild sexual integrity and win her back.* USA: Waterbrook Press, 2018.

Beall, Cindy, *Healing Your Marriage When Trust is Broken: Finding Forgiveness and Restoration.* Eugene, OR: Harvest House Publishers, 2011.

Beattie, Melody. *Codependent No More, How to Stop Controlling Others and Start Caring for Yourself.* USA: Hazelden, 1986, 1992.

Carnes, Patrick. *Out of the Shadows: Understanding Sexual Addiction.* Center City, Minn., Hazelden Publishing, 2001.

Cloud, Henry, and John Townsend. *Boundaries in Marriage.* Grand Rapids: Zondervan, 2002.

Crosse, Clay, Renee Crosse, and Mark Tabb. *I Surrender All: Rebuilding a Marriage Broken by Pornography.* Colorado Springs: NavPress, 2005.

Downing, Karla. *10 Lifesaving Principles for Women in Difficult Marriages.* Kansas City: Beacon Hill Press, 2013.

Grant, Elle. *Encyclopedia for the Betrayed: You're A-Z guide for anyone who's ever been lied to, cheated on & left for dead!* USA, 2018.

Gross, Craig and Clapp Logan, Chris. *The Volunteer's Back Pocket Guide to Sex: Guiding Teenagers on Issues from Pornography to Purity.* USA, 2012

Jenson, Kristen A. *Good Pictures Bad Pictures: Porn-Proofing Todays Young Kids.* Glen Cove Press, 2018.

Laaser, Debra. *Shattered Vows: Hope and Healing for Women Who Have Been Sexually Betrayed.* Grand Rapids: Zondervan, 2008.

Meyers, Joyce. *Battlefield of the Mind: Winning the Battle in Your Mind.* New York, NY, Warner Books, Inc. 2002.

Shanks, Shauna. *A Fierce Love: One Woman's Courageous Journey to Save Her Marriage.* Grand Rapids: Zondervan, 2017.

Stoeker, Fred, and Brenda Stoeker. *Every Heart Restored: A Wife's Guide to Healing in the Wake of a Husband's Sexual Sin.* Colorado Springs: WaterBrook Press, 2010.

Terkeurst, Lysa. *Uninvited: Living Loved When You Feel Less Than, Left Out, and Lonely.* Nashville: Thomas Nelson, 2016.

Thomas, Gary. *Sacred Marriage: What If God Designed Marriage to Make Us Holy More Than to Make Us Happy?* Grand Rapids: Zondervan, 2000.

Tidwell Palmer, Vicki. *Moving Beyond Betrayal: The 5-Step Boundary Solution for Partners of Sex Addicts.* Las Vegas: Central Recovery Press, 2016.

Websites
www.hilariebarry.com (women)
www.hopeafterbetrayal.com (women)
www.avenue.works (men or women)
www.180recover.com (men)

Acknowledgements

What an amazing journey this has been. I have gone from being a somewhat isolated woman with a very few friends and acquaintances, to a woman who can't begin to count all the people who have touched my life in profound ways. I have been truly blessed these past six years.

First, I want to thank my best friend, Joe. Even in our darkest moments you never left my side. Our marriage, now based in truth, was definitely worth fighting for. Thank you for loving me the way you do and for supporting me in writing this book. What a gift it has been to take our nightmare, Our Life Lesson, and create something that may help others grow closer to God and each other. Neither of us chose this journey, but there is no one else I would have wanted to travel it with. You are the bravest man I know. I guess that is because you are my sheep dog. I love you like no one else, Joe.

To our kids and in-law kids. We are so blessed to have all of you in our lives. Thank you for honoring our Family First motto and loving us even when we had to share hard truths. I am so proud of the amazing adults you have become, each so different and special in your own way. Thank you also for our eleven beautiful grandchildren and assorted grand-critters. We will never be bored with the adventures you bring our way.

Lorna, Geord, and Kenny, my siblings, isn't it amazing that you guys led me into God's light? I am so grateful you did. Now, I couldn't imagine this life without God or a past where I wasn't one of the four McKinnon kids. What a blessing Mom and Dad gave me, in you.

Thank you to our life group and larger Delaware Grace family, for leading us into a relationship with the Lord, teaching us the power of prayer, and trusting us with two challenging ministries. We are both grateful for the opportunity to help others as we were helped.

Vineyard Church, 180, Hearts Restored and marriage ministries, your policy of opening your doors to all broken people gave us the community we needed to get well and heal our marriage. I am forever grateful for all the people at Vineyard who invested in us.

John Doyel, what would we have done without you and 180? Your support of Joe and our marriage has blessed us and others by extension. Thank you for all you do to help men get well.

My dear friend Connie, thank you for hearing my story and sharing yours so I would know I wasn't alone. Hand in hand we will continue to become the women God calls us to be. I love you my friend.

Meg Wilson, your book was my hope after betrayal where I learned to identify the lies and look to God for His truth. You became my mentor when your ministry turned out to be a model for my desire to help others. I am so grateful for your example and friendship on this challenging journey.

Thank you to so many wonderful friends who read my early writing and encouraged me to keep pushing through, especially those of you who read my edited journals. Your kind words fueled my drive to move forward. And a special thank you to my editor friend who told me clearly that my edited journals were, "great material for a book, but definitely not a book." You put me on the path to learning to be a writer.

I am grateful to Cindy and Eddie and all the staff who make the Asheville Christian Writers Conference such a welcoming beginning for new writers. Thank you also for the opportunity to receive the Badge of Honor book award.

Larry Leech, thank you for holding my hand through the process of bringing my words to life. You were both writing coach and therapist as you gently encouraged me to revisit the difficult parts of my journey so I could share the emotion with my readers. You taught me to be a writer.

Jessica Brodie, thank you for bearing witness to my writer's journey starting at the Ashville conference when writing was brand new for me and ending here as my editor, giving me the confidence I needed to push the launch button. Thank you for all your hard work to polish my book.

Dawn Sturges, thank you for my beautiful cover and for the assurances you gave me throughout my extended writing time, that you would be with me when it came time to publish.

Brooke, thank you for all those evenings we spent getting to know each other and learning to create a website. I needed you by my side to fix my mistakes.

To all the women who have attended Infidelity Care for Women, formerly Hope and Healing. Thank you for trusting me with a piece of your journey and for being such a valuable part of mine. I pray that my book will bless hurting women as you have blessed me.

Lord, I am grateful you found me in the darkness and helped me understand that I am your Baby Girl and you will never leave me. As I move into this adventure of becoming a published author the words I hear are, "Trust me, Baby Girl." I will do that, always.

Follow Hilarie on Twitter (@hilbarry)
Join her Facebook group at Infidelity Care for Women
Read her writings at www.hilariebarry.com

Made in the USA
Monee, IL
02 June 2020

32401753R00142